P9-APD-390

Chicago's Urban Nature

Chicago's Urban Nature

A Guide to the City's Architecture + Landscape

SALLY A. KITT CHAPPELL

The University of Chicago Press | Chicago and London

SALLY A. KITT CHAPPELL, professor emerita of art history
at DePaul University, is the author of the award-winning
*Architecture and Planning of Graham, Anderson, Probst
and White, 1912–1936* and *Cahokia: Mirror of the Cosmos*,
both published by the University of Chicago Press, and a
contributor to the *New York Times* and other periodicals.

The University of Chicago Press, Chicago 60637
The University of Chicago Press, Ltd., London
© 2007 by University of Chicago
All rights reserved. Published 2007
Printed in China
For illustration credits, see page 237.

16 15 14 13 12 11 10 09 08 07   1 2 3 4 5

ISBN-13: 978-0-226-10139-2   (cloth)
ISBN-13: 978-0-226-10140-8   (paper)
ISBN-10: 0-226- 10139-8   (cloth)
ISBN-10: 0-226-10140-1   (paper)

This publication was supported by grants from the Graham
Foundation for Advanced Studies in the Fine Arts and the
Richard H. Driehaus Foundation.

Library of Congress Cataloging-in-Publication Data

Chappell, Sally Anderson.
    Chicago's urban nature : a guide to the city's architecture +
landscape / Sally A. Kitt Chappell.
        p. cm.
    Includes bibliographical references and index.
    ISBN-13: 978-0-226-10139-2 (cloth : alk. paper)
    ISBN-10: 0-226-10139-8 (cloth : alk. paper)
    ISBN-13: 978-0-226-10140-8 (pbk. : alk. paper)
    ISBN-10: 0-226-10140-1 (pbk. : alk. paper)
    1. Architecture—Illinois—Chicago—Guidebooks. 2.
Landscape architecture—Illinois—Chicago—Guidebooks. 3.
Parks—Illinois—Chicago—Guidebooks. 4. Chicago (Ill.)—
Buildings, structures, etc.—Guidebooks. 5. Chicago (Ill.)—
Guidebooks. I. Title.

NA735.C4C34 2007
720.9773'11—dc22

                                              2006033038

♾ The paper used in this publication meets the minimum
requirements of the American National Standard for Information
Sciences—Permanence of Paper for Printed Library Materials,
ANSI Z39.48-1992.

TO MY FAMILY: Especially my seventh great-grandfather, landscape architect John Reid, author of *The Scots Gard'ner* (1683);

My parents, William E. Anderson and Elinor Tanke Anderson;

My brothers and sisters;

My daughter, Jennifer Helen Chappell;

My son, Jonathan Claiborne Chappell, his wife, Mary, and their children Jennifer Marie Chappell, Katherine Elizabeth Chappell, Lauren Elaine Chappell, and Ryan Jonathan Chappell;

My son, David Lincoln Chappell, his wife, Heather, and their son Antonio Isaiah Chappell;

My husband, Walter Kitt.

Contents

CONTENTS

x

Maps

Acknowledgments

From the day I first decided to do this book I have been helped by others. My deepest debt is to cultural geographer Geri Weinstein-Bruenig, who engaged in a continually stimulating dialogue with me on every aspect of landscape architecture, urbanism, horticulture, and social philosophy. Many of the ideas were originally hers, and I accept them as gifts, for she gave them freely and often unprompted. On one occasion she called me from the steps of the New York Public Library to share a thought, on another from a parking lot in Milwaukee on her way to a class at the University of Wisconsin. She took me on walks through several of the major sites, offering her insightful criticisms. This book would not have been possible without her.

The benefits of collegiality in the architectural and landscape circles I am privileged to inhabit in Chicago are sustaining in more ways than I can say. Chief among these colleagues, I thank Robert Bruegmann, for his autonomy of vision, his perspicacious critique of the manuscript, and his supportive advice.

In addition to her lectures, books, exhibitions, and articles, Julia Sniderman Bachrach, archivist for the Chicago Park District, shared observations with me based on her deep knowledge of Chicago and its parks. It was a comfort to see her *The City in a Garden: A Photographic History of Chicago's Parks* on the shelf nearest my desk. I opened it nearly every day, always finding an accurate, indispensable account.

Jane Clarke, former education director of the Art Institute of Chicago and a distinguished author herself, has been a mentor in every aspect of the history of the Art Institute and Grant Park, and an invaluable advisor, colleague, and friend.

Another now well-worn work in my library is "Inventory and Evaluation of the Historic Parks of the City of Chicago" by John Vinci and Stephen Christy, with Phillip Hamp. Their thorough fieldwork and brilliant analyses, although written two decades ago and available only in xeroxed copies, were invaluable. Their maps saved me hours of time and served as guidelines for the site plans.

Years of reading the *Chicago Tribune* every morning have formed the basis of much of my knowledge about Chicago architecture. Blair Kamin, architecture critic, and Gary Washburn and Liam Ford, staff reporters, have done their work expertly, as have many others. They have filled me in and pointed the way on many local issues.

For help and advice generously given I am grateful to Lu Wallace, Kevin and Elaine Harrington, and a host of others in my architectural circles in Chicago. My friends William and Kathy Conger and Fred and Barbara Stafford spent part of a delightful dinner party evening asking me questions about the book and discussing my various working titles.

Volunteerism is a major force in bringing about needed changes and promoting stewardship of Chicago's public parks. In addition to their advocacy, members of Friends of the Parks, Friends of Lincoln Park, Open Lands, and Friends of the Chicago River have given generously of their time to answer my questions. Emese Wood, the late Glenn Steinberg, and I met every morning one spring to write "A Park Ethic," published in the *Lincoln Park Framework Plan.* These breakfast get-togethers also enriched my understanding of how changes can be brought about by dedicated volunteers.

Landscape architects and horticulturalists in Chicago invited me to their studios, opened their archives, and answered my many questions. My gratitude goes to Frank Clements, Joe Karr, Rory Klick, Michele McKay, Terry Ryan, Peter Schaudt, Ernie Wong, and Carol JH Yetken.

The staff at the University of Chicago Press has done invaluable work along the way. Susan Bielstein encouraged me with support and helpful criticism at every stage. Anthony Burton's patience and courtesy made all the days at my desk easier. Joel Score edited the manuscript with insightful consideration of substantive issues and organization as well as unfailing attention to the accuracy of details. Ryan Li's design work added beauty to every page.

Two interns from Smith College, Mary Beth Orr and Sara Abrams, and one from DePaul University, Michael LaCoste, did the field verification in the summer of 2005. Their careful work has made this a more accurate and helpful book.

Once again, I honor the services of librarians Doris Brown and Margaret Powers at DePaul University, Mary Woolever at the Art Institute of Chicago, Kathy Judge at the Chicago Botanic Garden, and Debbie Vaughan at the Chicago History Museum.

For any book involving publication of photographs financial support is crucial. Illustrations are indispensable evidence, especially for a text based on the thesis that architecture and landscape are mutually enhancing, that they are both at their best when fused into a single art.

Without support from the Graham Foundation for Advanced Studies in the Fine Arts and the Driehaus Foundation this book would not have been possible. I am grateful to the trustees of both institutions for their confidence.

My sons Jonathan and David are both writers, and their understanding has sustained me during the otherwise lonely business of writing. My two daughters-in-law, Mary and Heather, have lifted my spirits and blessed me with five grandchildren. At the heart of all my endeavors is the support I receive from my husband, Walter Kitt. He cheerfully drove me to all the sites, bringing companionship and offering insightful commentary along the way. His love is part of this book.

A Park Ethic

Parks connect us to the wider world of living beings and affirm the unity of our global environment. As gathering places for all people, parks increase our awareness of our common bond and nourish our democratic spirit. In parks we find relief from the tensions of daily life, through the relaxation provided by contact with green grass and trees, or through the exhilaration of physical exercise. The beauty of parks refreshes our senses and enables us to open our minds and our spirits. By preserving, managing, and caring for our parks we have an opportunity to cherish our legacy from the past, to enjoy the present and to leave a real and lasting benefit for the future. In order to realize this opportunity we will:

- Respect and preserve the delicately balanced order of nature;
- Recognize the obligation of a society to provide the beauty of open spaces and gardens for its people;
- Affirm the need of a people for landscape art as an inspiration for the continued growth of the spirit;
- Remember that parks belong to all of us, and respect the needs of others;
- Increase park space in our cities and provide for changing and diverse recreational needs;
- Support parks by voting for legislation to provide for their planning and funding;
- Translate our beliefs into actions through public, private and volunteer efforts to restore, maintain, preserve and improve our parks for future generations.

Sally A. Kitt Chappell, chair, Emese Wood, and Glenn Steinberg
Adopted by the Lincoln Park Steering Committee, June 4, 1991

Preface

There should not be two fields, architecture and landscape architecture. The design of building and landscape is one problem, therefore one solution.
—LOUIS KAHN

Architecture should swim in Nature.
—RENZO PIANO

Landscape is a powerful ideological framework for the construction of cultural values.
—DIANNE HARRIS

The manifest relationship between landscape and architecture in Chicago is the key to the city's success, yet the people who write about Chicago have not articulated, described, or even drawn attention to this vital dynamism at the heart of the city.

My early studies of architecture and landscape in Chicago left me feeling a strange void. Surrounded by mile after mile of skyscrapers, I felt an impoverishment of spirit. The world of office buildings and streets seemed too masculine—a widower's realm missing grace and ease. On the other hand, the historic parks and green spaces devoid of structural forms seemed too feminine—a widow's realm missing an energizing virile element. I found most satisfying those many places in Chicago where architecture and landscape were not only both present but where each had been conceived in response to the other, where the two had been created together as a single artistic whole.

Chicago is astonishingly rich in such combinations, and over the last few decades this dynamic relationship has evolved into a fusion that I call "urban nature." Sharing this perception with others is the goal of this book.

Each site that I discuss was selected because it has something to teach us about this urban paradigm. Accordingly, each entry plays a role in making this something more than an ordinary tourist's guide. It is a *pedagogical* guide as well, especially for those who seek to learn what Chicago can teach us about a higher form of city life.

One obstacle I found was that even the educated public has a narrow understanding of what landscape architecture is. Most people believe it is a special order of gardening, in which a professional selects and lays out trees, shrubs, and flowers for public parks or the estates of the wealthy. But landscape architecture is much more than this. Faced with a world where human beings have altered much of the earth's surface and even its atmosphere, today's landscape architects have manifold expertise: they are city planners who know how to integrate green space into the urban fabric; they are ecologists who understand regional hydrology, climatology, detoxification of contaminated sites, horticulture, and the history of their profession. They learn to conform to practices that help to maintain the delicately balanced order of the biosphere. The best landscape architects have a gift for fulfilling social needs and expressing human values in their art.

Among the places considered in this book are sites that demonstrate effective ways of connecting residen-tial buildings to each other and to the city (entries 41, Indian Boundary Park, and 65, Lake Meadows and Prairie Shores); places where streets and bridges become extensions of parks and links to each other (3, Michigan Avenue; 26, Wabash Plaza; 62, Drexel Boulevard; 46–48, Lincoln Park, a long linear park stretching five miles along Lake Shore Drive); industrial waterfronts that have become promenades or recreational areas (36, Calumet Park; 38, Harborside International Golf Course); sites set aside for education of the young (11, Soldier Field children's garden; 47, Peggy Notebaert Nature Museum; 57, North Lawndale Green Youth Farm); stretches of land that gracefully incorporate cultural institutions (8, Art Institute Gardens; 17, Navy Pier; 23, Washington Square Park; 48, Chicago History Museum); memorial settings (5, Cancer Survivor's Garden; 18, Olive Park; 43, Graceland Cemetery); generous plazas and walkways maintained by private corporations (6, Aon Plaza; 22, John Hancock Building Plaza; 25, Cityfront Plaza Concourse); former industrial sites turned community centers (14, Ping Tom Memorial Park; 39, Pullman); green roofs and ecological models for the future (2, City Hall roof garden; 53, Chicago Center for Green Technology); educational institutions that bring grace and felicity to the "town-gown" relationship (29, University of Illinois at

Chicago; 30, Illinois Institute of Technology; 34, University of Chicago; 44, DePaul University); restful lake views and secluded gardens (31, Promontory Point; 47, Alfred Caldwell Lily Pool); refuges for birds and other wildlife (32, Wooded Island in Jackson Park; 46, Magic Hedge at Montrose Beach); and places where Chicagoans can celebrate the democratic spirit of their city (4, Millennium Park; 48, Chicago History Museum). Readers interested in a particular type of building/landscape relationship, such as corporate campuses or multifamily housing units, will find further references in the index.

The old dichotomy between the worlds of the countryside and the city has been gradually dissolving, and Chicago has seen a merger of architecture and landscape that brings a whole new dimension to urban life, where people can have the best of both worlds. The process began in the nineteenth century and accelerated at the turn of the twentieth century. Some masterpieces from those earlier days remain and continue to manifest the benefits of a fusion of architecture and landscape. Garfield Park with its conservatory and Humboldt Park with its boat house, "receptory," and lagoons are exemplary. The process gained vigor in the late twentieth century as central city density decreased, factories and their pollution moved elsewhere, and public-private cooperation emerged to give the city a greener aspect. Millennium Park, with its fusion of nature and culture, is just one example among many.

Both architecture and landscape architecture are affirmative art forms. They are grounded in optimism, and their goal is to enhance human life. The affirmative nature of these art forms, and the process of selecting the best among them for a guidebook, inevitably gives this book a positive tone. Since I live here, I have long wanted to share the pleasures of Chicago with visitors and even with other Chicagoans who need a guide to explore unknown aspects of the city.

To keep the guide concise but meaningful, I have had to leave out some minor parks and small corporate plazas. My goal has been to give as much space to each location I do consider as it deserves, based not only on the significance of the design but also on size, longevity, plant materials, public appreciation, and social, historic, and economic considerations. I have also had to omit some of the criticisms I would like to level at the design community, especially my conviction that all young architects should have thorough training in landscape architecture and vice versa, eventually eliminating the distinction. Some of these ideas have found their way into articles for professional journals; others will have to wait for another book.

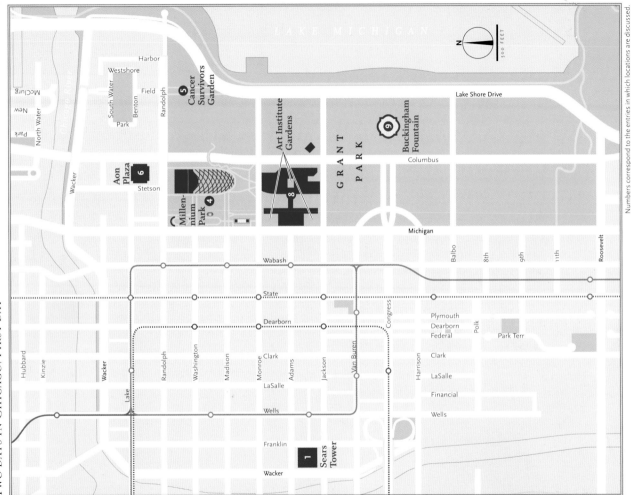

LAKE MICHIGAN

N

500 FEET

Numbers correspond to the entries in which locations are discussed.

Lake Shore Drive

Harbor

Westshore

South Water Park

Benton

Field

Randolph

McClurg

New

North Water

Park

Chicago River

Wacker

5 Cancer Survivors Garden

Art Institute Gardens

GRANT PARK

9 Buckingham Fountain

Columbus

6 Aon Plaza

Stetson

4 Millennium Park

8

Michigan

Wabash

State

Balbo

8th

9th

11th

Roosevelt

Dearborn

Plymouth

Dearborn

Federal

Park Terr

Congress

Polk

Clark

LaSalle

Financial

Wells

Hubbard

Kinzie

Wacker

Lake

Randolph

Washington

Madison

Monroe

Clark

Adams

Jackson

Van Buren

Harrison

LaSalle

Wells

Franklin

1 Sears Tower

Wacker

LAKE MICHIGAN

N
ONE MILE

Yates
Jeffery
62 Jackson Park
Stony Island

10 Museum Campus

Alfred Caldwell
Lily Pool
Café Brauer

Cottage Grove

Midway
Plaisance
61 Washington Park

King Dr

41

Michigan

State

Lincoln Park
Conservatory **47**

Broadway

Ping Tom
Memorial Park **17**

Halsted

35th
Pershing
43rd
47th
51st
Garfield
63rd
Marquette
71st

94 **90**

90

94

Clark

6th

Lincoln

Clybourn
Elston
Milwaukee

Ashland

Damen

Western

California

Archer

C H I C A G O

Humboldt Park
Boathouse

Humboldt Park
Formal Garden **52**

Grand

Central Park

94 **90**

Garfield Park
Conservatory **51**

Douglas Park **56**

Kedzie

55

31st

Lawrence
Montrose
Addison
Belmont
Diversey
Fullerton
Armitage

North
Division
Chicago

Lake
Madison

Roosevelt

Cermak
Ogden

Cicero
Laramie
Central
Austin

Pulaski

Irving Park

94

90

Columbus
Park **55**

MIDWAY
AIRPORT

Archer

In organizing the entries, I gave priority to geographic clusters, and convenience for the visitor, over historic continuity. Thus, Lincoln Park is discussed in part VI (North) and Jackson Park in part IV (South), although both are historically part of the boulevard system, which is mainly considered in part VII (West). Cross-references in the text should, however, make everything clear. Along the way I had to make up two words: *anthrostructure*, to describe the merger of two hand-built worlds, landscape and architecture, and *sculpitecture*, to describe the merger of sculpture and architecture. I have also used an existing word, *cosmopolis*," to describe a level of city development beyond the metropolis. As I use it, the term refers to an urban culture where the synthesis of the green world and the built environment is well established and the vision of this synthesis is widely shared among its leading citizens.

For Chicagoans, Professionals, and Visitors

I planned the book to be helpful to visitors, to people who live in Chicago, to armchair travelers, and to professionals in the fields of landscape, architecture, and planning. It should be readable on different levels. Those who want an overview can read the captions accompanying the illustrations as they are a précis of the text. The introduction offers an outline of the themes of the book. The entries are for self-guided tours, but armchair travelers can use the photographs as surrogates for a trip to come later. For professionals the book-length text itself is a sustained argument in favor of the merger of archiecture and landscape. In addition, professionals will profit from perusing the examples of any given topic as indicated in the table of contents or the index.

I hope Chicagoans will keep a copy in the glove compartment or backpack for weekend excursions, and read the text aloud to their families.

I advise visitors with limited time in Chicago to start with a visit to Sears Tower or the Hancock Building for an overview, and then spend the rest of the day walking along the lakefront, seeing Millennium Park, the Art Institute gardens, Buckingham Fountain, and the Museum Campus (all discussed in part I). If I had two days I would rent a car; visit Lincoln Park, with stops at the Alfred Caldwell Lily Pool, Peggy Notebaert Nature Museum, and Lincoln Park Conservatory (entry 47); then drive to Washington Park following the boulevard system (part VII). Along the boulevards Humboldt Park and Garfield Park have masterly combinations of architecture and landscape. Watching the sunset from one of the many places described in

Jackson Park (entry 32) would be a fitting climax to the "boulevard day." (See map on pages xxii–xxiii.) The third day should be devoted to special interests. Gardeners will not want to miss the Chicago Botanic Garden, people with children might choose Navy Pier, and history buffs may elect to spend the day in Pullman.

Two crucial caveats: landscapes are the most vulnerable of all urban art forms. In a short time they can be devastated by neglect, bad weather, vandalism, poor maintenance practices, too much or too little watering, harmful replanting, transplanting, insect infestation, and a host of other hazards. In just the five years I spent doing the fieldwork for this book I saw many areas disintegrate before my eyes. Some went from clean and charming to dirty and depressing; others were rescued from a neglected state and nearly miraculously restored. Now and then readers may need some imagination to see what I saw. To alert visitors to major changes, I will post important new changes on my Web site: http://sallyakittchappell.com. The need for both public and private stewardship on a constant and continuing basis became ever more obvious to me. I have learned to put an old American dictum to new use: eternal vigilance is the price of a healthy urban nature.

Theoretical Foundations and Methodologies

Although this is a guidebook, it is a guidebook that aspires to a higher level of the genre. It seeks to interpret the ways that architecture and landscape enhance each other when combined in a single setting so that readers and visitors will see the built environment in a new way. Instead of viewing spaces as negatives or voids, whether in parks or plazas, they will experience them as positive forces in the life of a city. Parks, plazas, gardens, and rooftops are culture-producing places, not merely places for retreat. Sidewalks and bridges become ends in themselves instead of just a means of getting from one place to another. It follows that Chicago is then a case study for principles that are applicable in cities worldwide.

Architectural and landscape historians are trained to verbalize what is essentially nonverbal, so that others may see more deeply into the meanings embodied in built forms. In recent years we have expanded our outlook and our methodologies. Now we endeavor not just to reveal meaning, but to study these spaces as embodiments of underlying social, economic, and political history.[1]

While I am firmly committed to the belief that there is no good practice without good theory, like other historians of my time I have found that no one theoretical position is sufficient for the work I want to do. Frederick Law Olmsted (that great American social theorist) saw that parks nurtured democracy, and his ideas formed the background of my thoughts on green spaces and social relations. At times an old-fashioned "aesthetic" or "stylistic" analysis helped me to put a site in context. More recent theories gave me new perspectives in varied ways. At times I looked at the world through a variety of "postmodern" lenses. In working on Millennium Park the new theoretical work on identity formation illuminated my thinking. I began to see that Chicago is consciously forming an image of itself as an ecologically up-to-date city in a culture-producing garden. Theories privileging space as an entity that can fashion knowledge and motivate political action were helpful in my analysis of Promontory Point. The new public-private sponsorships that have sprung up in Chicago are transforming power relationships with consequences we may perhaps not see for some time to come. Theories of the instrumentality of material form were helpful in opening my eyes to these connections.

For me, theories were a cabinet of different lenses and I tried to find the most clarifying one as I looked at each new problem. In addition I used a variety of methodologies. I am what Mario Carpo would call a "methodological eclectic."[2] At various times I borrowed techniques from cultural geographers, sociologists, botanists, historians, political scientists, urbanists, and others for fieldwork and interviews. In this sense the book is interdisciplinary.

Studies of urban nature are going on in many scholarly disciplines. No one can be a master of all that has been discovered in the last few years. At the outset I decided that my first step should be to lay the groundwork in Chicago and share it with others in the hope that help will be on the way for the work that remains to be done. A deeper look into the history of each of the sites chosen for this book, others that could not be included, and the overall picture, will no doubt reveal many connections I have not been able to see or articulate. The end of this book is not a conclusion but a commencement—graduating from one thing so that another may begin.

Finally, a reminder: Chicago has its share of big-city dangers, and people should exercise the usual precautions while exploring its parks and open spaces.

TASTE OF CHICAGO

Introduction
Chicago's Changing Paradigms

Since cities began, civic spaces have nurtured community spirit—the shared pasture, the marketplace, the city square. In Greece the agora gave birth to democracy. Greek citizens strolling beneath public colonnades on market days also debated political issues, argued over candidates, and criticized the performance of their elected officials. Outdoor theaters nurtured drama, art, and music. Philosophers and scientists sat on benches in gardens exchanging ideas. Priests performed religious ceremonies in sacred groves. Women gathered at the well, families and children at the seashore or the riverside. Today, all over the world, similar spaces continue to nourish public life.

In cooler climates, public space has also moved indoors. Domed statehouses have replaced outdoor meeting grounds. Cathedrals, concert halls, museums, department stores, and a host of other building types shelter religious, social, and economic activities in all weathers. As long as people had other contact with the natural world this was not a problem, but as cities grew more crowded, especially in the industrial era, the elimination of intimate contact with nature gave rise to feelings of deprivation—of separation from the earth. People no longer experienced the restorative power of seeing or being immersed in fresh water; they no longer witnessed the annual miracle of spring. As television, the Internet, cell phones, and other modern electronic devices have proliferated, the humanizing face-to-face contact with our fellow citizens has also diminished.

As one observer put it, "when the two-dimensional computer screen is becoming the dominant form of communication, people still seem to harbor a primal instinct to gather in real, live three-dimensional space."[3] To counteract the impoverishment of both private and public life, landscape architects, architects, city planners, enlightened business people, and visionary political leaders are now combining their efforts to restore our parks and plazas, streetscapes and waterfronts, and to forge new connections between the built environment and the natural environment. Contemporary designers of public spaces have increasingly focused on making "buildings interact with their surroundings rather than stand haughtily above them."[4] The 2006 winner of the Pritzker Architecture

Prize, the profession's highest honor, was one such designer, Paulo Mendes da Rocha, known for his Brazilian Sculpture Museum in Sao Paulo, where he treated the museum and the landscape as a whole, rather than creating just "a free-standing building resting on the site."[5]

Chicago is at the forefront of this international effort to expand and nurture civic life through a merger of public open spaces and civic institutions. In this new era, the green world becomes a vital part of the cultural meaning of the whole built environment. Parks and other open spaces are no longer an adjunct to city life, passive areas of retreat; rather, they are dynamic, culture-creating forces with documented health and social benefits. Integrating green spaces into the city creates a more interactive and humane environment, as Chicago's Millennium Park shows (fig. 1). One observer wrote:

> It was designed as a lush urban park, a star-lit concert space, a grassy art gallery dotted with high-toned creations, but Millennium Park has become something more. With approximately 3 million visitors streaming into the place last summer, with gospel and jazz and highbrow music set to sing again from its main stage . . . Millennium Park has become our town square, our meeting place, our focal point for the arts—at least when the winter winds aren't howling. . . . Yet in ways that perhaps even its planners hadn't

FIG. 1. With sparkling architecture and sculpture set among ribbons of green trees and grass, Millennium Park is emblematic of Chicago's urban nature, a merger of the natural world and cosmopolitan culture.

anticipated, Millennium Park has emerged unmatched in Chicago—and perhaps anywhere in the country—as a cultural nexus, a gathering place where rich and poor, connoisseurs and commoners, black and white and shades between bask in approximately 24 acres of music, dance, art, puppetry and whatnot.[6]

The great cities of the world—Rome, Paris, Istanbul, Petersburg, Beijing, and Kyoto, to name a few—have been doing this, each in its own way, for centuries. Each has attained a higher level of civilized life, has become what I call not a metropolis but a cosmopolis, a true city of the world. Chicago has now entered their ranks.

Ending the Dichotomy between Nature and Culture

In the past the city and the country were defined as opposites. Most people lived and worked five or six days a week in a grid of streets, houses, office buildings, factories, and warehouses. When the weekend came they went to movies, exhibitions, concerts and museums in the center of downtown, escaped to the country, or played and picnicked in a park. Life was divided into two unequal parts. It was an either-or world.

Today the goal is a both-and world, a city that encompasses within its own boundaries the benefits of country life. The schizoid split between the natural world and the man-made world is not acceptable. Urban nature is no longer an oxymoron.

Healing the split between architecture and landscape, or bridging the old gap between town and country, takes strong leadership and public-private cooperation. When the connection is made a new cityscape emerges—a place where people can have the best of both worlds in the same space, and sometimes, at the same time.

A New Perspective

As you gaze down at Chicago from the higher perspective of an airplane or a satellite photograph, the boundaries between the natural world and the built environment—between landscape, architecture, and infrastructure—are less distinct than they once were. Nature and culture, long regarded as opposites, are increasingly interwoven. Urban and suburban, too, are merging.

Close up, walking through the streets of the city, we see a new urban fabric that combines green, blue, and gray spaces. Buildings, highways, and parks can no longer be regarded as entirely separate. We see instead a dynamic whole, knit together by greenways and infrastructure. Each part influences and enriches the others. At some point in the greening of a city, as when thousands of new street trees were planted in Chicago, a critical mass is reached; the differences in degree add up to a difference in kind. Green spaces are no longer found just in set-aside parks but include sidewalks and streets. Bridges, especially those with pedestrian walkways, have become linear parks. Even former toxic waste sites have morphed into recreational areas, for example, the Harborside International Golf Course. Daniel Weinbach's landscaping at O'Hare and Midway airports welcomes visitors arriving in Chicago, bids a festive farewell to departing passengers, and greets those approaching the airports by car, taxi, or bus.

The kind of life most of us live in this amalgam, that I call our "anthrostructure," is qualitatively different from the life we lived as recently as twenty years ago. In the past, except for the Boulevard System, the street was the opposite of the park; today the landscaped street has become an extension of the park. Waterways that were once transportation conduits filled with industrial waste are now corridors lined with restaurants and cafés. And sidewalks have turned into miniature gardens.

Chicago's Path to Landscape Urbanism

In Chicago, landscape is not just places for pleasant parks, but a basic and fundamental part of the cityscape, including not just parks but sidewalks, streets, bridges, canal and river banks, and the lakeshore. It extends to front yards, backyards, temporary gardens on vacant lots, window boxes, lampposts, railroad and highway embankments, public squares, and even parking lots.

The waterways are especially significant. In addition to Lake Michigan, Chicago's water system consists of two pairs of rivers: the North and South branches of the Chicago River, which stem from a short east-west segment, and the almost parallel Grand and Little Calumet rivers, which merge to form the Calumet River. Man-made alterations—canals, lakes, and channels, piers, bridges, and related structures—are evident everywhere, especially in the southern part of the city. In the northern part, as a glance at a map will attest, forest preserves, parks, cemeteries, and golf courses form a nearly continuous greenbelt on the low-lying lands flanking the North Branch, from well beyond the city limits to just north of Addison.

The waterways, in particular the places where water meets land, have a long and complicated history. Since the first settler, Jean Baptiste Pointe DuSable, a man of French and African descent, built his log cabin near the mouth of the Chicago River in the 1770s, these areas have been highly desirable and their use hotly contested. The "battle for the lakefront" has been continuous and the subject of numerous books, as a glance at the bibliography in Lois Wille's superb book, *Forever Open, Clear, and Free: The Struggle for Chicago's Lakefront* shows.

One epic lakeshore struggle pitted Hyde Park residents against the United States Army Corps of Engineers and the Chicago Park District, which decided in the 1990s to grind up the massive limestone blocks protecting the shore from erosion to make a new type of barrier. The plan affected the entire lakefront, but only the citizens of Hyde Park, which includes the University of Chicago, organized to prevent the change, asserting the existing seawall's "deep historic, aesthetic and recreational value."[7] Chicago newspapers have also chronicled knock-down fights over convention center and stadium locations, marina designs, tree cutting for highway expansions, and regulation of bicycles, dogs, and skateboards. These struggles have often reached the Chicago City Council, the Illinois State Legislature, and even the Illinois Supreme Court.

Wille's book highlights the bitter conflict at the beginning of the twentieth century between Daniel Burnham, who envisioned parks as cultural places with museums and field houses, and Montgomery Ward, who favored open spaces. The debates over active versus passive use of parks and whether parks should serve as recreation centers or works of art, to be maintained according to their original design, continue to the present day, with vari-

ous civic organizations championing each view. They are part of a broader discussion of what landscape in the city should be.

In the 1960s and 1970s, the urban renewal era, the goal was to expand open space by putting huge landfills in the lake. Large parklike areas were placed between tall apartment buildings on Chicago's south side. Today the idea that a sharp distinction should be drawn between what is wild and what is a garden is countered by a growing emphasis on ecology and the use of native plant materials. At the same time, as park officials respond to community needs, deliberately "hybrid," multiuse spaces have become increasingly common in Chicago and throughout the United States. The same park may now contain a contemplative garden; grounds for baseball, tennis, soccer, golf, and other sports; a skateboard plaza; a dog run; a wetland preserve or set-aside wilderness area; a Saturday market square; a community center and auditorium; and other facilities.[8]

Chicago's built landscape recapitulates the history of major landscape and architectural movements from the eighteenth to the early twenty-first centuries. The city's parks include examples of Renaissance, picturesque, Prairie School, modern, and postmodern design. The formal gardens of Old Europe are visible in the carefully clipped hedges and crisp geometric flower beds, a la Versailles, in parts of Grant Park. Its classical balustrades, rostral columns, and terraces lend a continuing Beaux Arts air to Chicago's front yard. The picturesque tradition, begun in England, is reflected in the curving pathways, undulating hills, and decidedly informal layout of Jackson, Washington, and Lincoln parks, designed in part by Frederick Law Olmsted or his followers. The Midwest's own naturalistic Prairie style, celebrating indigenous plant materials is exemplified by the city's many Jens Jensen parks, notably Columbus Park on the west side.

One new park type, the small neighborhood park, was first introduced in Chicago at the turn of the twentieth century and quickly became world famous. Faced with problems of increased industrialization, crowding, immigrant populations, health issues, and other stresses, the South Park Commission hired the landscape architectural firm Olmsted Brothers and architect Daniel Burnham to design a whole new system of small neighborhood parks, soon nicknamed "Country Clubs for the Poor." Burnham invented a new multiuse building type, the field house, and the Olmsted Brothers worked carefully to unite landscaping and building. The field houses became community centers containing gyms, swimming pools, showers, theaters, craft studios, and branch libraries. Geometric regularity prevailed: the buildings were typically symmetrical, with a formal axis leading to rectilinear playgrounds and areas designated for specific sports—baseball, basketball, tennis, and soccer.

No longer was going to the park a substitute for a leisurely day in the country. The tranquility and unstructured spirit of the earlier, more passive landscaped parks was transformed by recreation directors, playground leaders, group workers, and a host of other new park employees. Trained to be instruments of social reform, they organized scheduled activities: classes, team sports, bicycle racing, chess and checker tournaments, dances, and a multitude of arts and crafts programs. The underlying belief was that parks could have the same beneficial social influences as Hull House, Jane Addams's public settlement house.

Unattended children were considered a threat to society, and providing proper activities for them was regarded as a means of instilling civic virtues and teaching correct social behavior. In the new field houses, paid leaders were expected not only to organize tournaments and pass out equipment but to serve as models of good conduct. This happened in many large cities in the United States between 1900 and 1930, a period Galen Cranz, in her excellent survey *The Politics of Park Design: A History of Urban Parks in America,* calls the Reform Era. "More ethics and good citizenship can be instilled into children by a play master in a single week than can be inculcated by Sunday school teachers and Fourth of July orators in a decade," noted a leading recreation theorist of the period.[9] Cranz herself spent the summer of 1969 designing playgrounds for Chicago's Neighborhood Improvement and Beautification (NIB) program, a federally funded open-space program. Part of the job entailed converting vacant lots into playgrounds and following through on older plans to construct playgrounds in larger parks.

The list of small neighborhood parks in Chicago is long, including McKinley, Sherman, Ogden, Palmer, Bessemer, Hamilton, Dvorak, and Avalon. A number of public squares also took form in this period, including Russell, Davis, Armour, Cornell and Mark White.

The importance of neighborhood parks cannot be overstated. Recent studies have shown that people appreciate simple green spaces that are close at hand even more than outstanding landscapes far from home. Having "nature nearby," where families can watch the crocuses emerge from the earth each spring, go for an after-supper walk on a summer evening, collect colorful leaves in the fall, or ice-skate in winter, is valued in almost all cultures.[10] These natural experiences, repeated year after year, are especially important for children. George Eliot put it beautifully:

> We could never have loved the earth so well if we had had no childhood in it,—if it were not the earth where the same flowers come up again every spring that we used to gather with our tiny fingers as we sat lisping to ourselves on the grass; the same hips and haws on the autumn hedgerows; the same redbreasts that we used to call "God's birds," because they did no harm to the precious crops. What novelty is worth that sweet monotony where everything is known, and *loved* because it is known?[11]

The neighborhood parks in Chicago are ordinary landscapes for ordinary people, a part of everyday life for hundreds of thousands, year in and year out, and the positive effects on personal growth, family cohesion, and community bonding are immeasurable. One person I interviewed told me this story:

> In the park across the street from our house my husband and I recently picnicked with our children. Just as we had settled in, a soccer ball landed in our potato salad! Soon a distraught looking father, with a soft Mexican accent, ran up, apologizing. My husband assured him that boys will be boys and the whole incident ended in smiles all around.[12]

A Tradition of Public-Private Cooperation

Enlightened businessmen in Chicago have participated actively in promoting large-scale urban enterprises for the public good since the city's early days. The greatest effort in the nineteenth century was the World's Columbian Exposition, the great White City or world's fair of 1893. The fair was a dazzling success. An ensemble of sparkling buildings, reflective lagoons, and countless plants and flowers, it attracted twenty million visitors in six months and vividly demonstrated what public-private cooperation and city planning could produce. The fervor it engendered carried over into succeeding decades. In 1906 the Merchants Club of Chicago told Daniel Burnham it would bear the costs of drafting a city plan for Chicago. In 1907 the Commercial Club joined the effort. Burnham worked with three subcommittees on the lakefront, the north-south boulevard link, and the location of railway and traction terminals. In the following year Burnham attended ninety-two meetings, working even on weekends. When the Plan of Chicago emerged in 1909 it embodied the spirit of a great city with a living goal that could bring its people together to make grand improvements in their urban environment.[13]

The same spirit carried over into a long succession of communal efforts, including the Century of Progress Exposition in 1933 and, most recently, Millennium Park. Those associated with the making of Millennium Park give businessman John Bryan and his committees much

of the credit for its success. It is widely acknowledged that Bryan is a part of a "long and essential chain of civic-minded Chicago business leaders who have helped turn dreams into reality."[14] The committees worked with mayoral appointee Ed Uhlir, a longtime Chicago Park District architect, who coordinated their efforts.

In the nineteenth century Chicago was a midwestern industrial center, in the twentieth a metropolitan city, and in the twenty-first it is becoming a cosmopolitan city. At the heart of these transformations, and of countless smaller changes and interactions, has been an optimistic belief in the whole city fabric as a democratic forum, a place where citizens and civic officials meet, mingle, express their values, argue, exchange ideas, and then cooperate.

Recent Developments, New Opportunities

Chicago is a variant of the merger of nature and culture visible in the world's most highly developed cities. Chicago is also a laboratory for a new kind of interactive landscape urbanism. If development continues as it has in recent years, with increasing interaction between the built environment and the natural world, a new "urban ecosystem" will dominate the future, and Chicago can serve as a model.

In recent years the importance of landscape architecture has also changed the face of corporate Chicago. Tax benefits and increased height allowances in exchange for providing public amenities at the ground level, along with design review, have produced many changes, both negative and positive. On the plus side, fountains, flower beds, new sculptures, walkways, and even an outdoor theater have sprouted around the perimeters of hundreds of skyscrapers and other business complexes. Neighborhood organizations and private homeowners have followed business's lead, planting roses, hollyhocks, sunflowers, and other colorful plants on railroad embankments, on sidewalk easements, and on the roofs of apartment buildings and single-family homes.

New green spaces have appeared everywhere—the median strips of boulevards, river embankments, old parks and squares, onetime traffic corridors, corporate campuses, educational and cultural institutions, and even on top of parking garages. Collectively the new green spaces connect the grays, tans, and whites of the skyscrapers, expressways, and houses, making a more gracious whole of these once disparate parts.

On the minus side, in some cases the increased height allowances have permitted buildings of almost gargantuan scale, with attendant problems of crowded sidewalks and traffic congestion. In addition, some developers have erected barriers, such as fences with gates or unfriendly "keep off" signage that make the public amenities seem more like private property.

The positive efforts, on the other hand, have helped elevate Chicago's reputation among park professionals. As recently as 2001 the Trust for the Public Land reported that Chicago was fifteenth out of the fifty most populous cities in the United States in amount of open space per thousand residents, behind Boston, Los Angeles, and New York. Los Angeles has 30,136 acres of parkland and New York has 36,646, but Chicago has only 11,729, about 0.41 acre for every hundred residents.[15] Chicago also ranked fifteenth in percentage of city area given over to open space, but it was twelfth in public expenditure on parkland, ahead of New York, Philadelphia, and Los Angeles.[16] Recent spending on Millennium Park may improve the latest expenditure figures.

The result is more than just a pretty spread, more than just a new civic aesthetic. It is a catalytic cultural change. The new spaces, and new connections with old buildings, have created new opportunities—economic, social, cultural, and educational. No longer opposed to each other, nature and culture are in symbiosis. Architecture and landscape reinforce each other, they reciprocate, each energizing the other. As the *New York Times* reported:

> By wrapping its arms and famous big shoulders around its Latin motto—Urbs in Horto (City in a Garden)—Chicago has become a global model for how a metropolis can pursue environmental goals to achieve economic success. During the last decade, the city's performance, measured in virtually every conventional category of civic well-being, has been off the charts, local boosters say. Chicago attracted more than 100,000 new residents, added tens of thousands of downtown jobs, prompted a high-rise housing boom, reduced poverty rates, built thousands of affordable homes, spurred a $9 billion-a-year visitor and convention industry, and transformed itself into one of the most beautiful cities in America.[17]

Just as important, the green spaces are culture-producing, generating stewardship for their own maintenance, helping to build community cohesion, and encouraging public-private partnerships, which in turn promote the culture-producing effects of the green space. A self-sustaining social chain reaction has occurred. Sometimes the benefits are more than self-sustaining, they are exponential, generating increasing benefits over time. When all goes well, all the players subordinate their goals to the greater good of the whole—the cityscape.

This is an anthrostructure in that both architecture and landscape architecture are shaped by human hands. We need a new term because these changes now reach beyond the conventional boundaries of the word *city,* and the old boundaries between city, suburbia, and exurbia are dissolving.

Three keys opened the possibility of this transformation in Chicago: vision, leadership, and communal effort. City employees credit Mayor Richard M. Daley for the initial vision. A few years ago, after a trip to Paris, the mayor asked a host of city agencies to begin cooperating with each other and with businessmen and private citizens in a collective effort to change the face of Chicago. Energized by his support, people in the Chicago Planning Department, the Department of Transportation, and the Chicago Park District initiated a series of programs, including CitySpace, NeighborSpace, and SchoolParks. As the various projects moved forward it became clear that the whole was more than the sum of the parts. The scale shifted from the urban core to a citywide fabric.

The Chicago Department of Transportation played a vital role in this metamorphosis. Providing design guidelines, information, and financial support, it assisted local businessmen, citizens' groups, neighborhood organizations, and aldermen in improving their neighborhood settings. New trees, plant materials, attractive street furniture, public art, historic markers, and other amenities were part of the mission of the city's Streetscape program. Recognizing that streets "form the grid that weaves the quilt of the city into a whole cloth," its Urban Design Program helped to promote the economic and social development of neighborhoods by renovating and improving the quality of their streetscapes. Creating a greener, friendlier environment for people is also closely linked to the goal of improving environmental quality.[18]

Changes in Chicago in turn influence and are connected to developments in "Chicagoland," which includes the collar-county suburbs, and beyond. And the surrounding region in turn influences Chicago. In recent decades, many people had moved to the suburbs to live, or to work in newly established "edge cities." Then, as the core of the city was revitalized, some of them moved back. Today rush hour on the expressways is congested in both directions, a nearly fifty-fifty split between traffic moving into and out of the city.

The Interaction of Social, Cultural, and Natural Experiences

In the new urban nature you are both close to the earth and in the heart of a large city. Trees spread their canopies overhead, you walk on lawns, you stand under a waterfall, but you also share the space and the pleasures with your fellow citizens.

Millennium Park is the city's best expression of this experience. When you sit on the grass listening to Mozart or Springsteen you become part of a cultural dynamic in which audience and musician each nourish the other's growth. As you walk back to your car from an outdoor art exhibition, you pass a sea of flowers waving in the breeze. No longer are the social, the cultural, and the natural mutually exclusive. The presence of each enriches the others, and each person leaves the park refreshed. Human beings have created this fusion. We have charged the natural world with social and cultural meanings. Why? Because, in our postindustrial world, we want the physical world to be home for all people, to celebrate our multifaceted human capacities. You can experience pleasure by yourself, but gathering together can transform pleasure into joy.

Neither the natural world nor the cultural world is enough. We want it all because we need it all. Cities are works of art, which societies create so people can find fulfillment close to where they live. In a dynamic cosmopolis this is an ever-growing, ever-changing process. As cities succeed, they increase their chances for longevity—witness the seven hills of Rome or green carpeted Kyoto.

In merging nature and culture the most successful cities combine such universal needs as maintaining or restoring contact with the cycles of nature, with specific, local characteristics. As you bask in the sun sipping coffee on the Champs-Elysées you sense at every moment that you are a part of Paris. Pausing on a stepping-stone to admire the reflection of a golden pavilion in a quiet pond distills Japanese culture for you in one image. The green hillsides of the Palatine overlooking the forum preserve the sense of classical history that is central to Roman identity.

Chicago's Uniqueness Celebrated

Various aspects of Chicago's unique identity are nurtured by the merging of its landscape and its architecture. The Fern Room in the Garfield Park Conservatory recalls a botanical past in the days before the great continents split apart, when the land that is now Chicago lay near the equator. Queen's Landing reminds us of Queen Elizabeth II's 1959 visit, Grant Park of the mass Pope John Paul II celebrated here in 1979. Buckingham Fountain evokes the majesty of Chicago's location on the Great Lakes. Humboldt Park offers an idyllic setting for *quinceañeras*, the coming-of-age celebrations held when Hispanic girls reach the age of fifteen. The Alfred Caldwell Lily Pool in Lincoln Park attests to the power of volunteerism and public-private cooperation in the restoration of landscape

treasures. The Prairie River in Columbus Park symbolizes midwestern roots. Ping Tom Memorial Park in Chinatown and the South Shore Cultural Center are gathering places for their respective Chinese and African-American communities.

Megaplanters on Michigan Avenue and other thoroughfares, from Irving Park Road to Indiana Boulevard, spread garlands of flowers throughout the city. Bridges and lampposts are adorned with hanging baskets. Benches, fences, water fountains, wastebaskets, and other street furniture sport new designs and fresh paint every season.

Enabling legislation has led business leaders to contribute to the greening of the city with such ground-level civic amenities as the Aon water cascade, Two Prudential Plaza, the Westin North Hotel's Garden; and the First National Bank Plaza.

The University of Chicago, the University of Illinois at Chicago, and the Illinois Institute of Technology have long graced their neighborhoods with the work of distinguished landscape architects. In recent years, other university administrators have also recognized the importance of pleasant outdoor spaces, flowering trees and shrubs, and other amenities in their environment, and have hired landscape architects to revitalize their landscape heritage and to create new green areas. The Chicago History Museum, Peggy Notebaert Nature Museum,

Museum of Science and Industry, Art Institute of Chicago, Shedd Aquarium, Field Museum, Adler Planetarium, and other cultural institutions have likewise hired teams of architects and landscape architects to give their buildings and their surroundings unity with each other and with the surrounding fabric of the city.

Opportunities for Social Cohesion and Tourism

Chicago's public officials recognize the importance of public events celebrating the uniqueness of the city. No effort is spared in promoting such annual events as Taste of Chicago, a ten-day salute to the veritable United Nations of restaurants within the city's borders (fig. 2), or Blues Fest and Jazz Fest, which honor Chicago's place in the history of American music. Just as important are the democratizing effects and community cohesion fostered by these massive gatherings. Ethnic diversity is always palpable and enjoyable in Grant Park, especially for the Fourth of July fireworks. An urbane courtesy emerges in the people crowded together on wall-to-wall picnic blankets. As Deborah Card, president of the Chicago Symphony Orchestra, puts it:

> Look out at the audiences that pack the Thursday night "Made in Chicago" jazz series, a multiracial throng that sways to Afro-Cuban backbeats one night, Eastern European folkloric melodies another, and you're seeing the face of Chicago, in all its hues. Listen to the languages—German, French, Spanish, Russian—that crackle before performances by the Grant Park Symphony and Chorus (which has nearly quadrupled its membership income since moving to Millennium Park in 2004) and you're hearing the cadences of a polyglot town. . . . It is this unique blend of ultra-high-end culture—everything done at the very highest level of quality in mind—yet its available to everybody.[19]

On a smaller scale, gatherings at such sites as Indian Boundary Park, the South Shore Cultural Center, and Humboldt Park facilitate social bonding within neighborhoods, as does the city's encouragement of local stewardship in neighborhood parks.

Thus a more cohesive physical fabric generates a host of benefits:

- *Producing culture.* Music, dance, the arts, and the humanities have more accessible and attractive venues.
- *Stimulating the economy.* Tax revenue from increased tourism bolsters the city's capacity to provide services.
- *Promoting social cohesion and enhancing democracy.* Shared, mutually enjoyable activities in pleasant

settings improve race relations and encourage democratic exchange.

- *Providing spiritual enrichment.* Access to recreational spaces makes it easier for office workers to take outdoor lunch breaks and creates opportunities for the greater population to renew both physical and spiritual strength.

In all these ways the merging of the urban and the natural acts to humanize the city and allay the stresses of urban life. The forces in this new kind of metropolis—a cosmopolis—are continually being shaped and reshaped as people set new goals and reach ever-wider populations. The process is as dynamic as the city life it serves to enhance.

FIG. 2. Taste of Chicago and other festivals draw thousands of people from dozens of ethnic groups to Grant Park. The urbane courtesy that typifies these gatherings demonstrates the democratizing benefits that flow from a "sense of place."

PART I

CENTRAL CHICAGO

The Emerald Crown

LAKE MICHIGAN

N
500 FEET

11 Northerly Island

5 Cancer Survivor's Garden

13 Burnham Park

10 Museum Campus

7 6 Aon Plaza

Two Prudential Plaza

Art Institute Gardens

6 Buckingham Fountain

Lake Shore Drive

G R A N T   P A R K

11 Soldier Field

15 Henry B. Clarke House/ Women's Park and Gardens

3 Michigan Avenue

4 Millennium Park

8

9

Columbus

Michigan

Michigan

State

State

12 Dearborn Park Neighborhood

LaSalle

Wacker

2 City Hall

Chicago

Wacker

1 Sears Tower

Lake

Congress

Roosevelt

Ping Tom Memorial Park **14**

Archer

18th

Cermak

1 Sears Tower Overview

233 South Wacker Drive (entrance on Jackson Boulevard)

To avoid waiting in line, buy advance tickets at www.theskydeck.com.

Show me another city so glad to be alive!
—CARL SANDBURG

Few cities can offer as awesome a sight as Chicago seen from the skydeck of the Sears Tower. The city spreads out before your eyes. At your feet the cool skyscrapers of the Loop anchor a dazzling mosaic of colors—to the east, the infinite blue of Lake Michigan; to the north, south, and west, myriad greens, brick reds, and limestone whites.

From this height, a quarter mile above the ground, a dynamic landscape appears. Thousands of white streets make up an underlying grid, holding everything together like stitches in a vast midwestern quilt. Here and there diagonals cross the fabric—rivers, parkways, expressways accented by cloverleafs, median strips, and bridges. Ecologically, this is still the Eastern Woodlands, and the millions of green trees—appearing like dots—and innumerable parks meld with the varied tones of the buildings into a soft viridian. Each direction affords a preview of an aspect

of the landscape urbanism of this cosmopolis whose motto is *Urbs in Horto*, the City in a Garden.

The eastern view is dazzling, one of the great urban vistas of the world. The blue of Chicago Harbor, framed by red-bricked Navy Pier on the north and the green of the Museum Campus on the south, sets off the array of jewels adorning Chicago's lakefront. Grant Park, the city's elegant front yard, lies between the lake and the Michigan Avenue streetscape, and contains the gardens of the Art Institute, Buckingham Fountain, the Monroe Harbor Promenade, Millennium Park, and the Cancer Survivor's Garden. The Burnham Yacht Harbor lies in the arms of Northerly Island, soon to be a nature center. Other highlights of the city's urban landscape are nearby. Newly developed private gardens further add to the sidewalk pleasures of citizens and visitors.

The northern view encompasses Lincoln Park, with its own sublime views of Lake Michigan. To the north and the south, lining both branches of the Chicago River, are green space developments: piers, terraces, boardwalks, landings, water-loving plants, and trees sprout on both banks of the old waterway in either direction, with industrial buildings more noticeable in the south.

Looking out the southern window one also sees, in the middle ground, Chinatown, with its enchanting Ping Tom Memorial Park. As far as the eye can see the waters of Lake Michigan meet the warm sand of Chicago's beaches and the parks at their borders.

Finally, the view to the west offers a handsome abstraction of the enormous urban grid, punctuated with suburban lawns and trees and the streets that give play to the movement of trucks and automobiles in a dynamic metropolis.

Landscaped Infrastructure

From atop the tower the visitor also gets a broad glimpse of the landscaping of Chicago's infrastructure, particularly along its major roadways—Lake Shore Drive to the east, the Boulevard System to the west—and the Y-shaped Chicago River.

During Richard J. Daley's mayoralty the traffic dividers on North Lake Shore Drive had deteriorated and the city planned to replace them with unadorned concrete "Jersey barriers." In one of the first efforts at beautifying the city, architect Walter Netsch, then a city park commissioner, persuaded the authorities to try a landscape solution instead. The median planters with trees and flowers installed at this time have delighted everyone ever since. The planters form a continuous line parallel to the blocks of buildings to the west, with gaps that allow for views of Lake Michigan at every intersection. Today old-fashioned flat-cup roses adorn the bases of the trees and, along with red, yellow, and orange daylilies, frame clear views of the blue horizon. On South Lake Shore Drive, where the lakeside park is sometimes very narrow, the city has had to erect large berms to protect the roadway from wave action during storm surges, so there can be no interruptions for views of the lake along this stretch. Still, the berms are attractively planted with curving beds of brightly colored flowers.

In the last decade a new version of the planters by landscape architect Douglas Hoerr has helped change the atmosphere of North Michigan Avenue and other boulevards throughout the metropolitan area (entry 3). Redesigning the embankment on the Chicago River is part of a comprehensive Chicago River Development Plan (see part III.)

Returning to the ground, a comparison of the Sears Tower and 331 South Wacker, the building across Jackson Boulevard to the south, is instructive. How does each building meet the street? The building to the south presents a gracious lawn, the Sears Tower a forbidding granite wall. The Sears Tower, designed by Skidmore, Owings & Merrill, was initially criticized for cutting off public access from the sidewalks, especially as the wall reaches a height of fifteen feet at Franklin Street. To answer this objection, a winter garden was added on Wacker Drive, though today, alas, the garden has been reduced to a security barrier.

By contrast, 331 South Wacker, by the firm Kohn Pedersen Fox, offers a wide, barrier-free lawn, a winter garden with café tables, and an indoor restaurant. The outdoor street furniture at 331 South Wacker is stylistically mixed, with Art Nouveau light fixtures and Adirondack chairs, but this quibble evaporates when one sees people enjoying their lunch hour on the lawn, under the dappled light of the honey locust trees. Inside, *Gem of the Lakes*, a large green figurative fountain by Raymond Kaskey, enlivens the winter garden, and bright bromeliads and other foliage adorn the bases of eight tall palm trees in the sunken court.

As with other indoor corporate plazas, the presence or absence of people determines the mood. At midday the place is vibrant. At four in the afternoon, nearly bare of people, the interior space, with its gray granite and gray marble pillars, may seem merely coolly elegant, appropriate only for a lone man in a business suit. Since the presence of people is vital to the success of a public place, making the environment at the base of a skyscraper attractive is crucial. But being attractive is not a complicated design problem—avoid barriers, have a lawn, flowers, shade, places to sit, and if possible a water feature, and the presence of people is assured. The works of great landscape architects are always welcome, but if they are not available, good, competent design, even with a few small errors, will go a long way toward guaranteeing success, as 331 South Wacker shows.

En route to City Hall, the exemplary Exxon Plaza (formerly First National Bank Plaza), at Madison and Dearborn, offers lunchtime musical entertainment during warm weather.

City Hall Roof Garden

Block bounded by LaSalle, Randolph, Clark, and Washington Streets

Open to small groups by appointment only. Call 312-744-5903 at least three days in advance.

Because dark surfaces, such as parking lots, absorb and radiate heat, temperatures in a city are as much as six to ten degrees higher than in surrounding rural areas. This phenomenon is called the "urban heat island" effect. Not only are the higher temperatures often uncomfortable; they also increase air-conditioning costs, add to pollution, and otherwise harm the environment. Chicago is one of the few cities participating in a U.S. Environmental Protection Agency program to help mitigate these problems—the Urban Heat Island Project.

A rooftop garden is one way to minimize the urban heat island effect. In the summer, vegetation reflects sunlight, provides shade, and helps cool the surrounding air through evaporation. In addition plants use excess carbon dioxide to produce oxygen, improving air quality. In the winter, the layer of soil provides insulation. Other benefits include absorbing storm water that would otherwise run off into the sewer system, and lowering heating and air-conditioning costs, a boon to tax payers in the case of government buildings. And improbable as it may seem,

even in the midst of a metropolis, a rooftop garden also attracts wildlife—bees, birds, and butterflies.

A pilot project on the roof of City Hall has already proved successful. Half of the building, which occupies a full downtown block, is managed by Cook County. The city has installed a garden on its half, and in hot weather the temperature directly below is several degrees lower than that under the county half's black tar roof, while in cold weather the city's side is several degrees warmer.

During the first few years the Illinois prairie specimens seemed out of place to neighbors in high-rise buildings overlooking the site, but carefully designed new plantings by the Conservation Design Forum have turned the surface into an intricate Persian carpet, with over 150 colorful species (fig. 3).

Success leads to success. On November 15, 2005, plans to give the Chicago Cultural Center a green roof were announced in the *Chicago Tribune*. About a third of the forty-five-thousand-square-foot roof will be turned into a garden with flowers, shrubs, and trees that bloom

FIG. 3. Like a flying carpet, the green roof atop City Hall offers people in surrounding buildings a view of a modern Paradise Garden. Meanwhile, scientific instruments collect data, allowing the city to advise other rooftop gardeners about what is most effective in Chicago's climate.

in different seasons. Sadhu Johnston, the city's environment commissioner, explained that "the roof was leaking and needed to be replaced, so it was a great opportunity to replace it with a green roof." There will be no direct public access to this garden, but it will be visible from the windows of surrounding residential towers and office buildings.[20]

The city has also published a pamphlet, "Chicago's Green Rooftops," that includes suggestions about weight, cost, design, irrigation, drainage, plant selection, growing media, maintenance, permits, and zoning requirements.[21]

The combination of living models and how-to publications has inspired the construction of hundreds of private roof gardens in the metropolitan area. From no green roofs in 1998, Chicago now has more than forty in public buildings, including one at the Chicago Center for Green Technology (entry 53). Private institutions, such as the Peggy Notebaert Nature Museum in Lincoln Park (entry 47), are also installing them, and a Chicago ordinance now requires that every new underground parking garage be built with a rooftop garden.

Michigan Avenue is emblematic of the changes that have transformed Chicago recently. The section north of the Chicago River, known as the Magnificent Mile, is dominated by skyscrapers on both sides. South of the river, between Randolph Street and Roosevelt Road, a panorama of famous Chicago buildings lining the west side of Michigan Avenue—the Chicago Cultural Center at the north end and, continuing south, the Gage Group, Orchestra Hall, the Railway Exchange, the Auditorium Building, and the Congress Hotel—faces Grant Park. The junction between this remarkable street wall and the park is now graced by elaborate floral displays. "Megaplanters" burgeoning with colorful flowers now decorate the median of downtown Michigan Avenue from the Water Tower south to Eleventh Street, mitigating the unpleasantness of the heavy traffic (fig. 4). Drivers and passengers in cars passing through—slowly during rush hour—or waiting to enter the parking garages under Grant Park, can enjoy the waving grasses and gentle flowers, while crowds of pedestrians on the sidewalks have an even better view.

FIG. 4. Decked with flowering shrubs and bright perennials, the megaplanters on Chicago's Magnificent Mile and other boulevards help humanize the city's streets.

In the early 1990s, landscape architect Douglas Hoerr received a commission to revitalize the landscaping, and other landscape architects have subsequently contributed to the design. Hoerr's idea was to create a more welcoming, humane atmosphere along Michigan Avenue, a pedestrian level experience that would soften the big city bluster and give a more gentle ambiance to the human space in between the buildings and the cars. The solution, heartily supported by the North Michigan Avenue Merchants Association, was both artful and economical, and its success has prompted merchants to add mini gardens on the easements between their own buildings and the curbs. At the time the program was initiated no one realized how much these joint efforts would affect the city and its future development through increased tourism and tax income.

Over the years Hoerr and other firms experimented with various plant combinations until they found designs bold enough to be enjoyed by people on tourist buses yet intricate enough to enchant daily passersby. Recently, some identifying labels have been added to inform the public of the popular and Latin names for many of the plants. Everyone—office workers, taxi drivers, visitors—loves these refreshing additions to the life of the city.

Behind the scenes the City of Chicago provides the infrastructure (planters, drainage, and soil), and local merchants fund planting and maintenance. When bulbs and other perennials are removed in the fall to protect them from winter salt, they are donated to outlying nonprofit groups. In the last ten years these plants have grown anew in neighborhoods all over the city.

Chicagoans have been inspired by Michigan Avenue, and countless other streets have sprouted similar colorful plantings, making the infrastructure of the city itself into a botanical urban amenity. The tone of Chicago is changing as more colors are added, the urban world and the natural world seem to be knitting together before our eyes. As winter turns to spring the whole urban fabric blossoms, and each season brings a new variation.

4 Millennium Park (Grant Park North)

East of Michigan Avenue between Randolph and Monroe Streets

See map on pages 28–29.

"Quintessentially millennial" might be the motto of Chicago's newest lakefront metamorphosis. To celebrate the turn of the twenty-first century Chicagoans turned 24.5 acres above an old railroad yard in an unsightly corner of Grant Park into a new model of urban nature. Working together for over six years, a group of public officials and private donors argued, held competitions, and finally made plans to make the emerging shared vision a reality.

At first the ideas for the new park were amorphous. When Chicagoan Cindy Pritzker, a major donor, was shown a Beaux Arts master plan for Millennium Park she asked, "For which millennium?" The template looked old-fashioned to her, and she wanted the new design to reflect the city's up-to-the-minute cultural life. Other donors shared her opinion. The challenge was daunting: giving physical form to the new twenty-first-century Chicago spirit.

Ed Uhlir, a long-time Chicago Park District architect, was Mayor Richard M. Daley's choice for project director. Uhlir drew up a program for the new park and invited artists from all over the world to present proposals. In ad-

dition he put local experts to work: landscape architects Terry Guen and Carol JH Yetkin on the overall plan, and Teng & Associates on the north garage. Guen designed the overall gentle topography that unifies the various areas of the park, with benches placed, like rests in music, to allow visitors to slow down and take in the impressions made by the art. Guen was also responsible for fulfilling Daley's wish for "four seasons beauty," selecting early-blooming pear trees for the spring and summer, "Autumn Blaze" maples for the fall, and evergreens for the winter along the borders of the park.[22] Uhlir himself coordinated the work with the Public Building Commission of Chicago, the Chicago Park District, and the Chicago Department of Transportation. By all accounts the chair of the Donors Committee, John Bryan, played a vital role throughout the whole process.

After the winners were chosen and work had begun, a nascent motive seemed to emerge: the desire to connect people's social and cultural interactions with the natural world. The various artists—landscape architects, architects,

Columbus

N
100 FEET

G

K

Aon Plaza

F

Stetson

J

H

MILLENNIUM PARK

I

J

Art Institute

Prudential Plaza

Randolph

E

C

D

B

A

Monroe

Michigan

MILLENNIUM PARK

A. Crown Fountain
B. McCormick Tribune Plaza
C. Cloud Gate
D. Wrigley Square
E. Chase Promenade
F. Harris Theater for Music and Dance
G. Bike Station
H. Pritzker Pavilion
I. Lurie Garden
J. Exelon Pavilions
K. BP Bridge

and sculptors—looked at Chicago, and apparently independently sensed the new civic atmosphere of the city. The result is a new genre we might call "sculpitecture."

SOCIAL INTERACTION. Contemporary Chicagoans wanted a true, democratic mixing ground, a public place to celebrate the city's diverse population working and playing together. A key feature of Millennium Park is that it allows us to share communal values and thus to create social bonds. As one visitor put it:

> When an African-American father sees me photographing my grandchildren on Frank Gehry's bridge and offers to take a picture with me in it, I hand him my camera and my thanks. I am grateful to the architect for bridging a social gap as well as a physical space. As a white grandmother, I feel good when I exchange smiles with a Mexican grandmother as our children frolic together in the Crown Fountain wading pool. I feel our democratic convictions finding expression. In a world where we are torn apart by conflict the world over, art can make the connections vital to our just getting along. [23]

CULTURAL INTERACTION. Chicago is the "City That Works," the "City of Big Shoulders," but also a city that creates. Chicagoans wanted to enlarge the city's civic image to acknowledge its dynamic cultural life. New ideas and social movements, new plays, music, architecture, sculpture, and other arts thrive in Chicago's nourishing environment, in the interaction of performers and spectators. Audiences support over one hundred experimental theater groups in the city, but a theater for intermediate size audiences, critical to the growth of young performing arts companies, was needed. The new Harris Theater for Music and Dance in Millennium Park, with fifteen hundred seats, fills the bill. At the other end of the scale, classical and jazz musicians play free concerts for over ten thousand people in the Pritzker Pavilion. In few other large cities in the United States can you find so many venues for the arts downtown, within walking distance of each other and close to hotels and transportation hubs.

INTERACTION WITH NATURE. The pleasures of being out of doors are abundant in Millennium Park. You can wade in water, watch a changing cloudscape, and smell roses. You can feel the earth beneath your feet, a fresh lake breeze on your cheek, and see fish dart in and out of reeds. You can escape to a bench in a quiet corner or along a promenade and read a favorite book during your lunch hour. These are all time-honored reasons that people go to parks.

But Millennium Park also offers new experiences, meeting the new needs of the twenty-first century. The list of new combinations is long: the synthesis of nature and culture, architecture and sculpture, landscape architecture and urban planning, contemplative spaces and facilities for large-scale events—all accomplished through exemplary public-private cooperation. But the combination is more than the sum of these parts. The end result is a paradigm shift in urban design: multiethnic, interactive land use in which a park is transformed from a merely passive, or recreational, space to a culture-producing civic institution.

add a friendly note that the older version—more memorial than living space—did not have.

Echoing Chicago's early Beaux Arts traditions, the peristyle reminds us that the phrase "Paris on the Lake" once embodied Burnham's vision of the city's future. Just as chestnuts line the Champs-Elysées, so does an allée of honey locusts line the walk on the northwestern edge of Millennium Park. Wrigley Square, a tree-lined room to the south, is also a transition to the adjacent ice skating rink and public restaurant, which continue in the classical mode, all warmed by the same yellow Joliet limestone, a signature stone of the Midwest.

Millennium Monument at Wrigley Square
Randolph Street and Michigan Avenue

In 1917 a stately classical peristyle, designed by Edward Bennett, the architect in Daniel Burnham's office who had worked on the 1909 Plan of Chicago, marked this corner of Grant Park. Today, in a slightly smaller version by the firm O'Donnell, Wicklund, Pigozzi and Peterson, pairs of Doric columns set on a plinth engraved with the names of the donors pay homage to the private contributors who helped make Millennium Park possible. Benches set near enough to a fountain to catch its cooling mists

McCormick Tribune Plaza and Ice Rink
Michigan Avenue, between Washington and Madison Streets

Graceful ice-skaters are beguiling figures in any winter scene. Bringing the sporting life to a frozen city they transform any space from cold to delightful. In the warmer months the rink, designed by Skidmore, Owings & Merrill, serves as a platform for jazz concerts and other events. Year-round it serves as a prime location for people watching; two cafés by the rink let visitors watch skaters and musicians against the backdrop of Chicago's famous Michigan Avenue buildings.

Jay Pritzker Pavilion

Frank Gehry's architectural/sculptural music pavilion is celebration itself. Exuberant metal curves 120 feet high crown the stage. A weblike trellis, six hundred feet long, supports a network of speakers, but that function appears subsidiary to its place-marking purpose. Beneath this open, seemingly organic roof are four thousand fixed seats and a grassy seating area the size of two football fields, with room for seven thousand more people. The lawn is gently sloped—not steeply raked—so picnicking is easy. If you cannot always see the stage you can still hear the music while you absorb the smell of the grass and the sight of the stars.

The pavilion and band shell together cost $60.3 million. The stage can be enclosed for cold weather use. It's an engaging place, bringing people, music, buildings, sky, and park together in a fresh harmony. Seated on the lawn you are at one with the people around you, the music, and the city. You feel enclosed and free at the same time.

Gehry's pavilion is not without faults. At this writing the acoustics are good in the middle section but need tweaking in other areas, and the obtrusive sound booth should be moved or modified. One also wishes that the view from Randolph and Michigan did not seem so "backstage."

On the whole, however, the pavilion transforms its part of Millennium Park and, more importantly, its part of Chicago. The festoons on Gehry's roof celebrate life in art-filled Chicago. The curling forms suggest the petals of a great flower, festive ribbons, a lion's mane, and even the undersides of cumulus clouds, all fitting metaphors for the various experiences the park provides.

BP Bridge

BP Bridge—a sensuous snakelike span also designed by Gehry—wiggles and twists over busy Columbus Drive, linking Daley Bicentennial Plaza, the Cancer Survivor's Garden (entry 5), and the eastern entrances to the parking garages under Millennium Park. The sleek tapered surface creates a breezy atmosphere, literally and figuratively, for the wind is deflected to "air-condition" the passageway. In addition, the sculptured walk provides gentle ups and downs, and twists and turns, giving people many different viewing angles during their approach to the park, comfortable overlooks on which to pause, and a wooden floor that meets the feet with a welcome softness. All in all, it is a grown-up toy of a bridge—strong enough to support hundreds of people and put them in a playful mood at the same time. Architecture has made fun of the snake, but no snake was ever so much fun.

Joan W. and Irving B. Harris Theater for Music and Dance

205 East Randolph Street

For years Chicago has needed a midsize theater for midsize music and dance companies, and the 1,525-seat Harris Theater, behind Gehry's pavilion at the north end of the park, fills the bill. Aboveground one sees only a "marquee," a transparent glass box that houses the upper portion of a multistory lobby and serves as a sort of entrance pavilion, and a rooftop terrace that will be used for such occasions as outdoor dining, exhibitions, and small concerts. Because lakefront ordinances prohibit any buildings in Grant Park, architects Hammond Beeby Rupert Ainge had to push the structure down thirty-five feet. (Two years later, Frank Gehry, aware of the problems, called his pavilion a "sculpture" rather than a building.) The theater shares rehearsal space, a loading dock, and other backstage facilities with the Gehry pavilion.

Visitors must go down several levels to get to their seats, but all difficulties of the passage are quickly forgotten when the onstage magic begins. Just two years after its founding the theater announced that the New York City Ballet will return to Chicago for the first time in twenty-six years to perform at the Harris. During the first year twelve companies agreed to use the theater; by 2006 the number was thirty-three.

Exelon Pavilions

Two smaller glass pavilions, also by Hammond Beeby Rupert Ainge, flank the Harris Theater and lead to other underground structures—the eastern one to the parking garage, the western to a visitor center, offices, and washrooms.

Corresponding pavilions at the south end of Millennium Park, on Monroe Street, were designed by Renzo Piano, who is also the architect for the new wing of the Art Institute, under construction across the street. With glowing solar panels on their roofs, and broad sparkling glass walls with thin limestone supports, these transparent structures show that a stairway to a parking garage can be beautiful. Acting as modern gazebos, they allow people to see through to the flowers and trees beyond. Millennium Park, after all, is the largest garage-roof garden in the United States. Plans for the new Art Institute wing also promise indoor-outdoor transparency and a bridge over Monroe Street to the park, resonating with Piano's belief that "architecture should swim in nature."

Lurie Garden

Monroe Street and Columbus Drive

If all grows well the perennials and trees in the Lurie Garden should reach maturity in a few years. At the opening in July 2004 the topography, the water feature, and the boardwalk were in place as was the massive formwork for the "Big Shoulder" hedge. The whole garden was designed by Seattle-based landscape architect Kathryn Gustafson and her firm Gustafson Guthrie Nichol, in collaboration with Piet Oudolf, from the Netherlands, and lighting designer Robert Israel, from Los Angeles.

The hedge will do double duty: it will shelter plants and people and set them apart from the hurly-burly of the other, busier areas of the park. This relatively quiet corner of the park brings welcome tranquility to a place where spectacular urban sculpture and architecture attract thousands.

Ensconced within the Big Shoulder hedge are a "light plate" and a "dark plate." The dark plate, to the east, will be tree covered, with shade-loving plants evoking the Chicago woodlands ecology; the light plate, to the west, already combines native and imported plants to suggest the brightness of the prairies. The interweaving of woodlands and prairies was characteristic of most of Illinois until the land was cleared for agriculture and corn, wheat, and soybeans took over.

By July 2005 the plants on the prairie side were mature enough to demonstrate one of Oudolf's most important precepts: No part of a garden should look wild. In keeping with this idea, Oudolf avoided the random inter-

mingling of plants found in natural prairies. Instead he grouped the plants in colonies for greater impact. Blazing star, bluestar, Northern sea oats, rattlesnake master, and coneflowers—each in its own cluster, together forming broad swatches of generous color over the softly undulating terrain.

The boardwalk that divides the two plates floats over water (fig. 5). It also follows the footprint of an old railroad retaining wall. The idea is to indicate what was once there, bringing the past to the surface of the present. The land here was once the Lake Michigan shoreline, later a landfill, then a railway yard, recently a parking lot, and now a garden above a parking garage. Whether the historical allusions will be too subtle for most visitors may depend on whether interpretive material is made available, but perhaps it does not matter. If the design provides aesthetic pleasure, the historic and metaphoric messages may be reserved for those who come repeatedly. Onetime visitors from out of town may enjoy the garden on one level, while Chicagoans and other repeat visitors will discover many different levels during different seasons of the year and over many years.

Eventually new gardens bordering on and within the new wing of the Art Institute will incorporate a rolling hedge that will unite them with the Lurie Gardens across the street. This hedge, together with new streetscaping on

FIG. 5. On a hot day, visitors to the Lurie Garden boardwalk in Millennium Park can dip their feet in the water at a spot that was once the Lake Michigan shoreline. Other historic allusions include an homage to Carl Sandburg—the "Big Shoulder" hedge.

both Monroe and Randolph Streets, will unify Grant Park with Chicago's grid. And when the final touches of lighting designer Robert Israel are added, the garden will glow with nighttime magic.

Bike Station

Randolph Street and Columbus Drive

Can a bike station be beautiful? Can it be a convincing example of the merits of green architecture? The idea of encouraging people to bike to the Loop is itself part of the energy-saving ethic of the new "green architecture" movement, but this small structure by architects Muller & Muller carries the idea to a new dimension. Solar panels conserve electricity, while the cables that secure the exterior will soon be covered with vines. Within there is space for three hundred bikes, a repair shop, locker rooms and showers, and offices for the Chicago Police Department's bike patrol. Bright blue awnings provide shade in keeping with the spirit of the great lawn of the park.

Chase Promenade

The green canopy over the promenade separating the busy western half of the park from the quieter section to the east is a welcome relief. Although there are plans to fill the broad walkway with tents for special activities, perhaps as time elapses park officials will decide there is already quite enough going on and let the promenade be what a promenade has always been—a place to walk. As designed by architects Skidmore, Owings & Merrill and completed by McDonough Associates, the space, although a little wide, is now a fitting setting for a quiet Sunday stroll.

Cloud Gate
SBC Plaza, between Washington and Madison Streets

Taxi drivers, small children, elite collectors, and art critics all agree—*Cloud Gate* is a triumph. Even before the park opened to the public, Anish Kapoor's sculpture was an ingenious focal point, bringing together the sky, the great buildings on Michigan Avenue, and the landscape. But those of us who watched it go up were astonished at what a difference the presence of visitors made once the park opened (fig. 6). When people started streaming in it became much more than a mirror of its surroundings—it sprang to life with symbolic value.

As people pass beneath its curving form, *Cloud Gate* seems to give birth to a huge family, uniting people of all races, colors, and creeds in the wonder of a shared moment in a special place—under the sculpture, under the skyscrapers of Chicago, under a midwestern sky. It is thrilling, and one of those rare natural highs only public art can give.

I can think of only a few other places in the world where this happens. It happens in Chichen Itza at the equinox, twice a year if it isn't too cloudy. It happens in Venice at the annual Feast of the Redeemer. It happens at the parade of the dragons in Japan and during Holi in India, when celebrants fling colored powder at one another. It happened the world over at the celebrations marking the turn of the millennium; a progression of images shown on public television captured Aboriginal dancers emerging from the surf to drum beats on the beaches of Australia, then moved to record fifty-seven simultaneous weddings by the pyramids of Egypt, and finally caught the countdown of the digital clock at Times Square.

Now a communal celebration happens in Chicago every summer day, and sometimes during the cooler months. On one level, it is just plain fun to be under *Cloud Gate*. Like a good circus it beguiles "children of all ages". Another level appeals to the erotic—the forms, like so much of Kapoor's work, suggest breasts and buttocks, and you don't have to be a Freudian to sense womblike contours as well. The artist expresses the public and the primal. Here is the place to celebrate being alive and together in Chicago, a feeling architects call a "sense of place."

FIG. 6. *Cloud Gate* gathers people from all over the world—and the Chicago skyline—in one reflection.

The work's name is appropriate. *Cloud Gate* acts as a city gate. It also shelters and unites us within enclosed space—reflections of people, skyscrapers, and the lake are all enclosed in an ever-changing cloudscape—and therefore is architecture. But its symbolic or expressive content moves beyond the structure, into feelings that are usually only evoked by sculpture. Like the work of some other artists of the twenty-first century—James Turrell or Michael Heizer, to name just two—this sculpitecture manifests the best of both art forms. Although the final cost was more than two and a half times the original budget, most Chicagoans think it was worth it.

Crown Fountain

Monroe Drive and Michigan Avenue

Video images of the friendly faces of two Chicagoans rise on two fifty-foot towers at the southwest corner of Millennium Park (fig. 1). Across a black granite reflecting pool, they smile at you, they smile at each other. Then the towers turn magically into sparkling waterfalls and every twenty minutes spout jets of water over eagerly waiting children screeching with joy. The colorful lights change, two new faces appear, the water show repeats itself, and the children screech with joy, again and again and again. In the middle of the pool, which is covered by only an inch

of water, barefoot grown-ups join the children. Like the video faces above them, they are black, white, yellow, and red, young, middle-aged, and old, rich and poor. Instead of celebrating kings and queens, generals on horseback, or the mythological figures of the Old World, this fountain celebrates the democracy of the New World, in one of democracy's quintessential cities—Chicago. Most significantly, it transforms the way a great city sees itself: as a dynamic work of art. Designed by Spanish sculptor Jaume Plensa and executed by Chicago architects Krueck & Sexton the fountain seems to say, "Come on in, the joy is for everyone."

The fountain and its urban plaza invite participation, without which it is incomplete, just as people are incomplete without public celebrations. We need the irresistible allure of art to magnetize a crowd, to turn it into a group, and art can sometimes deliver on the promise. It does so in the Crown Fountain. Even in fall and winter, when the water is turned off, the lighting vitalizes the space.

Just a year after its completion it was clear that Millennium Park was not only a success as a new kind of green space but also an economic engine in the Loop. Like properties bordering New York's Central Park, condominiums being built or converted on Michigan Avenue have skyrocketed in value. Developers' list prices for the area have jumped from $383 to $483 per square foot since the park's completion. Views of the park, as well as the perception that the views will not be blocked in the future, account for only part of the rise. Other factors include the value of the location as a status symbol, and the amenities that are springing up nearby to accommodate an estimated 2.5 million new visitors a year. According to Louis D. Angelo, president of Metropolitan Properties, "The success of the park has created an explosion of demand. Clearly, the area has been revitalized into a 24/7 neighborhood. The East Loop is now much more vibrant and inviting than it was 10 years ago." Increases in tax revenue are also mounting.[24]

Is Millennium Park perfect? Of course not. Critics have rightly complained that the artworks are jarringly separate entities, that they have no aesthetic connection with each other. In addition, they are not ideally sited in relation to the park as a whole, or to the city on its border. Some have voiced regret that the park seems to have no overall unity, that the connective infrastructure, with its Beaux Arts ramps and balustrades fails to bring everything together and is itself out of place with the more modern designs of the rest of the park. Landscape experts worry that some of the metaphorical implications of the Lurie Garden, such as the Big Shoulder hedge, are weak and unconvincing.

Other critics have said that Millennium Park is a theme park, but it is not. It has some of the magic of a theme park for children, but the real works of art within Millennium Park have expressive content for adults. Theme parks are hodgepodge copies of Old World antiques, made of lath and plaster and usually at a reduced scale. Visitors are expected, above all else, to spend money.

Here, by contrast, four world renowned artists, Frank Gehry, Jaume Plensa, Anish Kapoor, and Kathryn Gustafson, together with a powerful team of Chicago's finest landscape architects and architects, have expressed the spirit of Chicago as it enters a new millennium: bold, innovative, democratic, and beautiful. The artworks are unique, the materials of the highest quality, the sense of place genuinely and uniquely Chicago. The scale is not merely full but genuinely grand, well fitted to the skyscrapers and Lake Michigan that are its frame. Even children sense the difference, just as they know the difference between a Styrofoam Easter egg and a real one. No suspension of disbelief is necessary here. In the final analysis, balancing the pluses and minuses, Millennium Park is a success—a democratic new model for a new millennium. The impact is fully authentic.

5 Cancer Survivor's Garden

337 East Randolph Street

A delicate filigreed pavilion frames the entrance of the Chicago's Cancer Survivor's Garden. Set between two monumental Corinthian columns, it is the portal to a spiritual journey (fig. 7). Plaques placed along the pathway bear messages attesting to the survivability of cancer:

> "There are treatments for every type of cancer."
> "Seek and accept support."

The entrance pavilion is on the uppermost of four terraces. Beyond it, a stairway descends to the second terrace, a broad flower bed, followed by the third terrace, a long, rectangular green lawn marked by urns and lined with benches. The fourth terrace contains a plaza with a view to the south. Above sunlight filters through allées of crab apple trees on either side, further emphasizing the climactic vista—down Lake Shore Drive to the temple front of the Field Museum of Natural History, with the infinite blue of Lake Michigan beyond.

The sequence of vistas might be metaphorically associated with either survival or reconciliation with mortality.

This poetic ambiguity is a major expressive achievement for the designers, but the garden is not the masterpiece it might have been. It is undeniably a popular success. In the summer months, for instance, I have seen many bridal parties drive up in limousines to be photographed in the Cancer Survivor's Garden. (Though when I discretely asked the photographers if anyone in the group was a cancer survivor, three out of four times the answer was "no"—they had chosen the place for its beauty alone.)

This is one of twenty-six Cancer Survivor's Gardens in the United States and may well be the most beautiful. Its aesthetic success, however, is limited by its funder's extensive requirements. Richard Bloch, one of the founders of H & R Block, established the R. A. Bloch Cancer Foundation with his wife Annette after surviving, through aggressive treatment, what he had initially been told was terminal cancer. The foundation's mission is to spread the word that cancer is survivable. Among other programs, it provides grants of up to a million dollars to construct gardens in cities with populations over one million (with lesser amounts available for smaller cities). The

grants, however, are subject to extensive and stringent programmatic requirements: Each garden must have an "Acceptance Plaza," a "Triumphal Arch," a "Positive Mental Attitude Walk," a "Garden of Names," and a "Celebration Area," as well as twenty-three signs of various sizes, a sculpture, and a computer so visiting survivors can add their names to an online registry.

Propagating the idea that cancer is survivable is a laudable public service. One only wishes someone could persuade the foundation to give designers a freer hand.

The Chicago Park District designers—architects Miriam Gusevitch, Julie Gross, and Ron Salazar and landscape architect James Slater—did find creative ways to satisfy some of the requirements. The filigreed arch in the entrance pavilion, part of the Acceptance Plaza, is their answer to the triumphal arch requirement. They also substituted the double allée of crab apple trees for the Garden of Names and placed the computer in a low box at the end of the Celebration Area overlooking Lake Shore Drive. (In 2006, alas, the computer was not working, and the surrounding area was filled with debris.)

FIG. 7. Set on an axis with the classical temple facade of the Field Museum in the distance, the entrance to the Cancer Survivor's Garden is monumental—a fitting start to a spiritual passage.

Originally the designers also planned a reflecting pool where the lawn now stands. What an effect this pool would have had! Mirroring the sky, echoing the murmur of the passing breezes, sweetening the air, and softening somewhat the symmetry of the layout. In five additional strokes of powerful poetic metaphor, they called for beds of medicinal herbs, rows of juniper trees, a butterfly garden, and a cascading water feature, and for putting the texts for the signs in the Positive Mental Attitude Walk on the bases of urns filled with seasonal flowers.

Unfortunately Bloch vetoed the water feature. The medicinal plant area at the north end of the garden and the butterfly garden at the south end, between two small end pavilions, also never materialized. And the texts were not put on the bases of the urns but on separate, unnecessarily assertive plaques between the urns, where they add only intrusive and inappropriate staccato notes. Of these five features, only the juniper trees were included, and to this day they provide a certain evergreen stateliness to the walkways.

Four taunting losses. Taunting because they could still be manifested! The texts could still be placed on the bases of the urns, the lawn turned into a pool, the medicinal herb bed planted, and forbs that attract butterflies added. Attracting butterflies would be easier than it might seem. The park is on the annual migration path of monarch butterflies as they fly south for the winter. The poetic image of hundreds of them emerging into the southern sky seemed to the designers a perfect finale to the experience of the Cancer Survivor's Garden, as it alludes to the process of transformation and could apply either to healing or to reconciliation.

It is true that this migration only occurs during the fall, but thousands of people travel thousands of miles to see other annual events—the sun entering a slender window in a Native American cave wall at the vernal equinox, or the snake king descending the pyramid at Chichen Itza, to give just two examples. With a fitting setting for the butterfly migration, Chicago might have had an artwork of this order, as well as a major tourist attraction.

(There was also one fortunate omission. Chicago law requires all sculpture in public parks to be approved by the Chicago Fine Arts Commission, and the commission rejected a rather garish sculpture that had been suggested.)

Finally, this garden raises more profound issues. Designers should be free to determine their expressive focus, especially in a garden that deals with cancer. In Chicago the focus is on renewal—renewal as a return to health or renewal as transformation through reconciliation to mortality. In other cities the template ruled out the latter interpretation. Indeed, American culture overall tends to deny death. But when you deny mortality you preclude transformation through reconciliation. One of the Blochs' plaques reads, "There are ten million living Americans who have been diagnosed with cancer. Three million are considered cured." What does that imply about the other seven million? In the face of these statistics, a celebration solely of surviving not only denies death but borders on triumphalism.

In Chicago the designers created a poetic space, both healing and consoling, and welcoming not only to survivors of cancer but to people who have accepted that they are terminally ill and to the families and other survivors of those lost to cancer. It needs only a few restorations to celebrate its potential as a meaningful work of art.

Across Randolph Street from the garden entrance is North Field Boulevard, which leads to a new park in the Lakeshore East development.

6 Aon Plaza
200 East Randolph Street

When you walk down the stairs from Randolph Street to the Aon Plaza (or use the entrance pavilion elevators, which facilitate handicapped access) you leave behind the noise of cars and traffic and enter a world of almost Baroque splendor. Jets of water arc through the air in front of you as great cascades fall behind you (fig. 8). Within this magical atmosphere employees take their coffee breaks, and visitors picnic on polished benches under shady trees. The plash of water even muffles people talking on their cell phones.

Movable gates at the east and west ends of the central fountain open to let people get wet if they like. On a hot day you can stick your hand in one of the jets and splash water on your face, arms, and neck to cool off the way the Romans have since ancient times. Originally commissioned by Amoco, the complex is now owned by Aon Corporation. The pavilion was designed by Voy Medeskies of Holabird & Root, the fountain and garden by Jacobs/Ryan Associates.

FIG. 8. A refreshing sunken garden, with a circular pool and a cascade, is accessible by elevator or stairs at Aon Plaza, just off Randolph Street. A city ordinance gives corporations the right to build higher if they provide a public amenity at street level.

7 Two Prudential Plaza

130 East Randolph (entrance on Lake Street)

Here the whole is more than the sum of its parts. The original forty-one-story Prudential Building, erected in the 1950s, rises alongside a sixty-four-story skyscraper built in the 1990s. The towers are joined at the lobby level, and an outdoor plaza designed to unite the old and the new creates a welcoming sense of civilized urbanity. The arrangement took advantage of a Chicago ordinance that allows buildings to go higher if they have public amenities at the ground level.

The formality is urbane, reminiscent of a corner of the Tuilleries, but the design features more colorful plantings than its Parisian predecessor (fig. 9). The complex, by architects Loebl Schlossman & Hackl, has two fountains, each with four jets that emerge from circular pools and are illuminated at night with submersible fixtures. The jets in the upper fountain splash into a circular pool and then flow down through semicircular cascades to the

FIG. 9. Elaborate water displays refresh the atmosphere at Two Prudential Plaza. The walls of the surrounding skyscrapers protect this "outdoor room," which buzzes with visitors all day long in warm weather.

lower pool. In just one acre, flowers, water, and places to sit mingle. The parterre garden sits at the center of a promenade; on the outside edges long granite benches offer a place to stop and rest. To soften the effect of the granite, the designer planted shrubs and a small grove of trees on either side. Each tree has recessed up-lighting, and small lights are added during the holidays.[25]

With water playing in pools beside formal rectangular beds of begonias, petunias, and other annuals in red, orange, yellow, white, and blue, there is also a hint of Versailles in this corporate corner of Chicago. The allusion reminds us that, in the Beaux Arts days of the 1893 world's fair, Chicago was often called "Paris by the Lake."

The Art Institute of Chicago has several gardens beckoning from spaces enclosed by its various wings—the South Garden, the Stanley McCormick Memorial Garden (or North Garden), the McKinlock Court Garden Restaurant, and the East Garden, currently being redeveloped to fit into the new Renzo Piano addition.

South Garden

Michigan Avenue between Adams and Jackson Boulevard

The first landscape architect in Chicago to give life to the idea of a continuous flow between building, garden, and street was Dan Kiley, and he first gave the idea form in the South Garden of the Art Institute in the mid-1960s. Kiley always tried to relate his gardens to the adjacent buildings and to the surrounding city, as this superb urban design shows.

Entering from Michigan Avenue we see Lorado Taft's *Fountain of the Great Lakes* (1913) rising beyond a grid of cockspur hawthorns, just as Lake Michigan rises beyond the grid of Chicago's streets (fig. 10). Few monuments

express the spirit of a city on the Great Lakes as well as this. (Buckingham Fountain, a few blocks to the south, and Santiago Calatrava's Milwaukee Art Museum are its only rivals.) The axial relationship of the buildings and the plant materials shows Kiley's sensitivity to the Beaux Arts spirit of the Art Institute, this section of Grant Park, and Chicago's dominant urban pattern. The symmetry also gives a sense of harmony to the ensemble and contributes to the calm inspired by the garden.

One goes down a few steps as one enters this sunken garden, which in itself imparts a new dimension to the experience of city life. We can step away from noise and confusion, sit down under the protective shade of trees, have lunch, and socialize with friends for a while. The denseness of the trees gives the space an enclosed feeling—it is a welcoming outdoor room.

A reflecting pool and a few low jets form a fountain complex against the west wall of the museum's Morton Wing, adding the refreshing sound and smell of water and mirroring the leafy canopy and the sky overhead.

The row of tall honey locust trees at street level on

Michigan Avenue, echoed by honey locusts against the wall on either side of the fountain, enhances the connections between the city and the Art Institute and at the same time marks a separation. Kiley placed the shallow-rooted trees (beneath the garden is a parking garage) in granite planters that are just the right height for sitting, and specified crushed stone for the walkways because it sounds better underfoot than gravel.

The axial organization of the garden facilitates an easy walk through the series of spaces the visitor encounters: from a true Beaux Arts promenade under the tall trees along Michigan Avenue, down into the more intimate grid of hawthorns, now adorned by vines and flowers at their borders, and across to the climax, the reflecting pool and Taft's sculpture, against the leafy relief of the honey locust trees.

Kiley was a pupil of Warren H. Manning, who in turn was a pupil of Frederick Law Olmsted. Kiley is thus heir to a long line of "philosophers of the land," to use his term for Manning. Kiley also believed in architect Louis Kahn's dictum "There should not be two fields, architecture and landscape architecture. The design of building and landscape is one problem, therefore one solution, therefore one person." Through its gardens the Art Institute becomes at one with the larger urbanity reflected in Chicago's motto, *Urbs in Horto.*[26]

North Garden

Monroe Street and Michigan Avenue

To enter the North Garden is to enter a different world. For many midwesterners it is a more familiar world—a spacious lawn, edged on the north with colorful flowers, recalling the backyard gardens of the cities of the plains (fig. 11). Compared to the serene and elegant world of the South Garden, the North Garden is busy and active.

The 1991 design by Hanna/Olin preserves the great elm trees on the west, which provide a leafy canopy and welcome shade in Chicago summers. The handsome, humungous, but harmless *Flying Dragon*, a vivid red sculpture by Alexander Calder, seems at home in the grass, as do other sculptures by David Smith and Henry Moore. A long line of tall purple alums make an architectonic segue to the balustrade of the terrace along the northern wing of the Art Institute, where students and visitors often sit, rest, read, or watch the passing panorama. A colony of river birches in the southwest corner is thriving, as are

FIG. 10. Architecture, sculpture, and landscape unite in this masterpiece, Dan Kiley's urbane South Garden at the Art Institute. Inviting people to descend into a quieter world, the symmetrical layout also connects them to the grid of Chicago streets and leads them to the symbolic *Fountain of the Great Lakes*, by Lorado Taft.

FIG. 11. Playful sculpture and plantings enliven the North Garden of the Art Institute, where students and art lovers lounge on the lawn from April to October.

McKinlock Court Garden Restaurant

The McKinlock Court Garden Restaurant at the Art Institute is one of Chicago's Beaux Arts delights (fig. 12). Enclosed by spacious arcades on all sides, the garden is reminiscent of the courtyards of Renaissance palaces, and indeed of all classical architecture. In summer the café section is bordered by neatly clipped hedges, with dozens of festive silver tables and chairs protected by soft green umbrellas. The pool emits sparkles of blue, and splashes of water suffuse the air with tinkling sounds. Green, blue, and silver—these are Great Lakes colors, and the four playful mermen of Carl Milles's *Triton Fountain* capture the spirit with their spouting fish and seashells held aloft in the dappled light under six stately elm trees. The two most beautiful words in the English language, said Henry James, are "summer afternoon," and that mood is embodied here.

the well-established honey locusts. It is a garden for sunny seasons, whereas the South Garden is for all seasons.[27]

The Michigan Avenue gardens make the Art Institute a genial Chicago resident, and the "well-maintained, landscaped gardens in front of the wings, in addition to providing a welcome oasis in the city, also help in setting off admirably the main building. . . . The ensemble possesses a unity and serenity that would be the envy of most urban museums."[28]

Fig. 12. Lunch in the McKinlock Court Garden Restaurant at the Art Institute makes any day in June a rare day.

East Garden
Monroe Street and Columbus Drive

A water sculpture by Isamu Noguchi and the gateway from the old Chicago Stock Exchange, the Louis Sullivan building that once occupied the site, sit in a narrow garden on the east side of the Art Institute. The museum's new northern wing, designed by Renzo Piano, will include a bridge tying it to Millennium Park and a new garden by Gustafson Guthrie Nichol, intended as a further visual connection to the park across the street. There will also be a new courtyard garden behind the south wall of the new building. The architects describe it as "an outdoor room or gallery, uniting interior and exterior spaces. It will be fully visible at the first floor through the glass facades of the internal 'main street' or concourse of the addition. Ginkgo trees to the east will connect the courtyard with the streetscape of Columbus Drive and Grant Park."

Buckingham Fountain (Grant Park South)

Between Columbus and Lake Shore Drives, at Congress Drive

With its jets soaring high into the air and cascades of exuberant water falling to fill basin after basin, Buckingham Fountain symbolizes the Great Lakes as does no other work of art on their shores (fig. 13). Expressing the power of these majestic waters and their metropolitan capital, Chicago, the fountain and its surrounding gardens were selected as a fitting welcoming place for Queen Elizabeth II when she arrived by royal yacht in 1959. (The adjacent point on the lakeshore is called Queen's Landing.) Bordered by colorful flowers, it is the crown jewel of Chicago's landscape architectural heritage.

The fountain is also the centerpiece of Grant Park, Chicago's formal front yard. Inspired by the Bassin de Latone in Versailles, it embodies the French Beaux Arts legacy, but is twice the size of the original. When they designed it in 1927, architects Bennett, Parsons, and Frost, with sculptor Marcel Francois Loyau and engineer Jacques Lambert, must have reasoned that the fountain needed to be grand in scale. Its background on the west is the skyline of Chicago, on the east the infinite stretches of Lake Michigan. Close up, the pink Georgian marbles of its contours sparkle in the sunlight and are illuminated by magical colored lights on summer evenings. To make the picture complete, playful bronze sea horses gambol in the waters, symbolizing bordering states. Seen through jets of water the skyscrapers of Chicago seem inviting in the background.

This area of Grant Park is also Chicago's premier outdoor gathering place. Huge crowds can be accommodated on its lawns. It was here, in 1979, that the city received Pope John Paul II. More mundane festivals such as the annual Taste of Chicago, Blues Fest, and Fourth of July concerts and fireworks also take place here. A cosmopolitan city can entertain the world as well as its own citizens.

A skateboard park is planned for the intersection of Balbo Drive and Columbus Drive. When it is installed it should let visitors from more sedate parts of the world enjoy watching the antics of Chicago's young daredevils as they gnarl around the ramps and bowls of this latter-day playground.

FIG. 13. By night or by day, Buckingham Fountain continues the Beaux Arts tradition that once earned Chicago the nickname "Paris by the Lake."

In their 1909 Plan for Chicago Daniel Burnham and Edward Bennett envisioned a "cultural arc" of formal gardens and cultural institutions between the city and Lake Michigan. Although the museums were not built exactly where the two architects imagined them, this cultural arc now extends from the Chicago Cultural Center, at Randolph and Michigan, through the Art Institute, Orchestra Hall, and the Auditorium Building, and on to the Field Museum, the Shedd Aquarium, and the Adler Planetarium.

When the Field Museum was erected in 1921 it was not placed at Congress Avenue as Burnham intended, but at Roosevelt Road. Here it was at the center of a divided Lake Shore Drive. In those early automobile days, the view from a touring car on a leisurely drive was part of an urban motoring expedition. It made sense to see the Field Museum—on its elevated base, central to the conception of Grant Park as a Beaux Arts design—as the end point of an excursion, from both the south and the north. As time went on, of course, traffic increased, and drivers enjoyed the vista in peril of their lives. Worse yet, going overground from the Field to the Shedd or the Adler, east

of the drive on the lakefront, involved crossing eight lanes of speeding traffic.

To solve these problems, Lake Shore Drive was reconfigured in the 1990s, with all lanes now to the west of the Field Museum, and the team of landscape architects John MacManus (then of the Chicago Park District) and Lawrence Halprin (based in San Francisco) and the firm Teng & Associates produced a new concept plan for the area around the museums. The end result of their efforts is that the museums are not only more closely connected with each other but also more cohesively integrated into Grant Park and the fabric of the city.

The highly lauded design of the new Museum Campus is both historical and contemporary, formal and informal, practical and beautiful.[29] The great lawn at its north end aptly complements the monumental presence of the three museums. Approaching the new terrace of the Field Museum, we feel ourselves part of a larger whole, at one with the spirit of a metropolis; looking back from that terrace, we see the skyscrapers of the Loop and Lake Michigan (fig. 14).

FIG. 14. The skyscrapers on Michigan Avenue and Randolph Street join with Lake Michigan to frame one of Chicago's finest expressions of urban nature—the Museum Campus. Meandering paths take strollers from one museum to another, back to the city, or on to the nearest bench to admire the flowers or the view.

From all directions the museum complex is now the climax of one of the world's great urban vistas. Just as the Louvre sounds the coda of the Champs- Elysées in Paris, or the Victor Emmanuel Monument crowns the Via del Corso in Rome, so the new Museum Campus gives monumental form to South Lake Shore Drive.[30]

The approach to the Museum Campus along South Lake Shore Drive is lined with magnificent elm trees, like great goblets reaching sixty or seventy feet into the air. The grassy embankment leading down to the water has a double promenade of crab apple trees and is separated from Lake Shore Drive by a berm that softens and nearly mutes the noise of the traffic. Since people on wheels have separate paths, pedestrians needn't fear being mowed down by cyclists or roller bladers, and the latter are free to enjoy the wind in their hair as they glance at the sailboats to the east.

Visitors approaching from the north along the lakeshore climb a ramp to enter the forecourt of the Shedd Aquarium and come upon cascading grass terraces. These act as a foreground to the very formal neoclassical forecourt of the Field Museum. It seems the setting has the best of both possible worlds: it echoes the geometry of the museums and the city, but includes the natural world of grass, trees, and water.

At this writing the plantings are not yet complete, and here and there the campus feels like an empty canvas, but plans are in place for further development. All in all, however, it is clear that the spirit of the Burnham Plan has been carried forward into a new age. Burnham himself would surely have approved.

11 Soldier Field and Northerly Island (Burnham Park North)
425 East McFetridge Drive

One of the first areas of Burnham Park to be redeveloped was the heavily used space around Soldier Field (fig. 15). When plans were announced for an addition to the stadium, designed in the 1920s by Holabird & Roche, the city promised the development of seventeen new acres of lakefront parkland. As the addition by Lohan Caprile Goettsch was going up in 2002, landscape architect Peter Lindsay Schaudt began work on designs for the new park.

Faced with the challenges of integrating two enormous parking garages, Schaudt created some dramatic topography, a magical Children's Garden, a broad lawn for picnics, a new memorial for veterans, and a winter sledding hill. North of the stadium, on McFetridge Drive, the visitor sees gardens, planted with groves of American lindens and male ginkgo trees (female ginkgos have an unpleasant smelling fruit). A monument and a fountain

FIG. 15. Tailgate picnicking takes on a new meaning for people coming to Soldier Field's new parkland. Seventeen acres of grassy lawns, playgrounds, and a sledding hill greet after-game revelers and casual visitors. The nearby Children's Garden is a spiral of educational opportunities.

wall, dedicated to members of the armed services, mark the northwest entrance to the stadium, continuing the arena's original commemorative tradition. The ground cover, in planters, is of horsetail grass, a primitive plant, which, like the ginkgo, survived the ice age.

Children's Garden

Just east of Soldier Field, the Children's Garden is as rich in meaning and symbols as it is in opportunities for outdoor play. The nautilus spiral of the path is fun to follow, even if allusions to the fossil shells in the Field Museum, the sea horse tails in the Shedd Aquarium, and representations of the Milky Way in the Adler Planetarium are lost on younger children. There are numerous ways to learn from the artful sculptures here: by hiking up the *Climbing Earth,* touching the *Rock Earth,* manipulating the *Water Earth.* The cast bronze *Geography Earth* uses small symbols to indicate cities in the world on the same latitude or longitude as Chicago, and these are repeated along the path.

If you can tear yourself away from the Children's Garden, a walk down the path to the east and south leads to a splendid view of the Burnham Yacht Harbor and Northerly Island. Further on, the great lawn invites before- or

after-game picnickers to spread their blankets under some old American elm trees.

Schaudt has contoured the land over the two garages so successfully that all sharp edges are blurred. When mature the honey locusts and maple trees planted on top of the garage will contribute their leafy canopies to the view, and their shade to the garage roof (which is made partially of structural foam to reduce weight).

With its setting of evergreen, lilacs, and roses, the Gold Star Memorial area is an appropriate place for those who have lost loved ones in the line of duty. A winter garden is planned for the area to the south. For now, the sledding hill marks the end of the park.

Northerly Island (formerly Meigs Field).
Solidarity Drive and Lake Michigan

Northerly Island was first developed between 1928 and 1930 as the site for the 1933 Century of Progress Exposition. The Plan of Chicago of 1909 illustrates Daniel Burnham's dream of a chain of man-made islands off the lakeshore, but the landfill here is the only one to be realized, and not in the way Burnham envisioned.

For many years after the world's fair, Northerly Island was the site of a small airport serving small planes and commuters primarily traveling between Chicago and Springfield, the state capital. In March 2003, Mayor Richard M. Daley ordered city workers to Meigs Field in the middle of the night to destroy the lone runway before dawn. As an advocate of more urban green space, Daley had long wanted to turn the airfield into a park. In press conferences the next day, he cited the threat of terrorism as another motive for his action.

Plans are now underway to develop a nature center for children, with bird walks and other family activities to be developed on the site. Rotary International, founded in Chicago in 1905, has agreed to plant a garden behind the Twelfth Street beach house, in honor of its centennial. From 2005 to 2007, and perhaps beyond, a temporary summer entertainment venue was set up by San Antonio–based Clear Channel Entertainment. The Chicago Park District expects this concert venue to generate money to help pay for the future nature park. The opening-night performance by the bands Earth, Wind and Fire and Chicago drew a near capacity crowd.

12 Dearborn Park Neighborhood

Bounded by Polk Street on the north, Eighteenth Street on the south, State Street on the east, and Clark Street on the west.

One of the nation's most successful urban renewal projects, Dearborn Park (fig. 16) bridges the Chicago Loop and South Loop neighborhoods. The area was once filled by railroad infrastructure and printing businesses that grew up around it. But between 1950 and 1970, it was largely abandoned. In 1975 a group of Chicago business owners acquired twenty-four acres for development. A key feature of their plan, which included three high-rise buildings with a total of 803 condominiums and 166 town houses, was an extensive landscape plan. Play lots, jogging trails, two parks, swimming pools, tennis courts, tree-lined streets, and other amenities completely changed the character of South State Street. Lois Wille wrote:

> Dearborn Park left a formula that other cities can use to turn fallow land into vibrant communities, and without big subsidies. It involves shared investment and shared risk on the part of local businesses and local government. It tempers political and social ideology with practicality and

marketability. And it requires the grit and guts and civic spirit that built Dearborn Park.[31]

The success of Dearborn Park played a large part in spurring other developments in the South Loop. To date, more than $1.4 billion has been invested in the neighborhood, most of it after 1983, when it became clear that Dearborn Park would be a success. Landscaping played a critical role in transforming the area from a derelict industrial site to a verdant community. Tree-lined sidewalks and abundant greenery brought the foliage of the suburbs to the heart of downtown Chicago. Residents felt they had the best of both possible worlds.

Daniel Weinbach, the landscape architect, specified pink and white flowering crab apples, birches, clusters of bright maples and oaks, honey locusts with their transparent foliage, and hearty lindens. All plants were chosen for proven adaptability to city life and ability to handle pollution and midwestern freeze-thaw cycles. In marked contrast to the landscaping at Lake Meadows (entry 65), where the undulating topography is a reminder of Corbusier's idea of placing high-rise apartment buildings in parklike settings, the tree-lined streets and small gardens here follow the grid of urban Chicago. The street grid, disrupted by railroads, was restored, and small pocket parks were fit into the new pattern.[32] Although very different in design, the landscaping at the two complexes has been an important, if often overlooked, factor in the success of both. It also helps mitigate the "State Street wall," with its overhead el tracks, which tends to cut the development off from its surroundings on one side.

Several Chicago architectural firms participated in designing the various parts of Dearborn Park, including Skidmore, Owings & Merrill, Booth Nagle & Hartray, Pappageorge/Haymes, Barton Associates, Ezra Gordon/ Jack Levin, Fitzgerald and Associates, Michael Realmuto, and Dubin, Dubin, Black & Moutoussamy.

FIG. 16. Nestled between Grant Park and an expanse of old railroad tracks now planted over with trees, grass, and flowers, Dearborn Park has the best of both worlds—proximity to downtown, and the greenery of the suburbs.

13 Burnham Park Central

Between Lake Shore Drive and Lake Michigan, from Twenty-third Street to Fifty-fifth Street

For parking, exit Lake Shore Drive at Oakwood Boulevard and turn east.

In 1999 the Chicago Park District commissioned the Burnham Park Framework Plan to develop this narrow stretch of lakefront parkland from McCormick Place south to Promontory Point (entry 31). At present, the main attractions are its views of the city and access to Lake Michigan. The natural dune setting is also a good place to read, relax, or meditate. Here you can climb down onto great pier rocks and find a perch perfectly suited to your mood—out of the water or halfway in, level or on a slant, near other people or in solitude. The pier rocks, however, are an endangered heritage. They have been replaced for miles along the lakefront with swaths of solid concrete intended to protect the shoreline. (The Army Corps of Engineers ground up the rocks and used them as aggregate in its concrete.) One key exception is at Promontory Point, where community activists blocked the change. Other parts of Burnham Park have play lots, a model yacht basin, basketball courts, and other athletic facilities.

Plans are now being implemented to improve Burnham Park at many levels: new pedestrian bridges over Lake Shore Drive to connect the park to adjacent communities, a new beach, new community center/beach houses for various activities, and a comprehensive system of site furnishing to give cohesion to the whole.

14 Ping Tom Memorial Park

300 West Nineteenth Street, at the South Branch of the Chicago River

Ping Tom Memorial Park, in Chicago's Chinatown, is a microcosm of the nature-culture symbiosis at work in the larger city. It is also a neighborhood park par excellence. The site was a former railroad switching yard, a linear mass of tracks hemmed in on all sides by other urban infrastructure—an elevated-rail segment of the Chicago Transit Authority's Orange Line; the South Branch of the Chicago River; an automobile bridge crossing the river on Eighteenth Street, which at present marks the north end of the park; and at the park's west end, an industrial age lift bridge, now used for a Metra commuter train crossing. The CTA Red Line and a second Metra line can be seen to the east.

The park gives life to these iron, concrete, and steel elements, which not only are made acceptable as background but even contribute formally and historically to the cultural overtones of the park. The park and the surrounding neighborhood thus *become* each other, in both senses of the word. Chinatown is a historic urban node within Chicago's industrial past, and the park makes this relationship mutually revealing and appealing (fig. 17).

During the design process, landscape architect Ernie C. Wong, principal of Site Design Group, involved the community of older immigrants, business owners, and members of the younger generation. Through the participatory process Chicago's Chinese population began to feel that this public space belonged to them. Landscape architects know that such engagement is a precondition of the public stewardship of parkland that must persist after the design is implemented. If the park is to thrive, the people who use it must continue to take care of it after the designers have done their work.

In good condition today, the park attracts people from other parts of Chicago on a daily basis, increasing tourist income. No longer do people go to Chinatown just to eat. Instead the park has made the whole area a cultural destination. *Sink, Sank, Sunk,* an outdoor performance by the experimental theater group Red Moon, attracted thousands for evening performances in the summer of 2004. Students from surrounding schools and colleges often select Ping Tom Memorial Park as a term paper

FIG. 17. Giving expression to the communal life of Chicago's Chinese community in the space between an overhead highway and an industrial lift bridge was the challenge facing landscape architect Ernie C. Wong, the designer of Ping Tom Memorial Park.

topic. Local children delight in the playground equipment. Everyone finds there is a lot to see besides the architecture and sculpture in the park: long freight trains, the astonishing lift bridge, fishermen casting their rods, and a variety of boats plying the river.

Older immigrants will recognize the adaptation of an ancient Chinese landscape principle: the traditional succession of walled courtyards is transformed into a succession of open courts. First comes an airy Entrance Plaza, marked by the Four Dragon Gateway. Now a popular place for senior citizens and their morning tai chi chuan exercises, it is defined by rows of flowering ornamental trees. The edges also frame the view of the next space, the Riverfront Pavilion. With its curved roof and festive yellow and red décor, the pavilion resembles a pagoda, creating a strong sense of Asian place. It has become a focus for community events, such as a Sichuan dance recital and a concert by local Chinese musicians.

To the Chinese, nature equals mountains and water, and therefore rocks and water are essential symbolic elements in all Chinese gardens. The stroll garden at the south edge of Ping Tom Memorial Park satisfies this need, but the big rocks that articulate the space are also as at home in the Midwest as glacial erratics. Visitors strolling in the garden seem happily at ease in the lively urbanity on all sides.

When the flashing silver streaks of Metra or Amtrak trains pass through the lift bridge downstream, or pleasure boats ripple the reflections of a nearby industrial warehouse before docking at the park, it all seems part of some yin-yang fusion of nature and culture. To think that watching a vertical lift bridge raise its enormous span to let a flotilla of barges, sailboats, yachts, and canoes pass underneath would be the spectacle served up to an audience in a Chinese garden!

The park is dedicated to Ping Tom, a Chinatown real estate developer who transformed thirty-two acres of the adjacent rail yard land into a new residential and commercial area, and who was also active in the formation of the park. It also reflects Mayor Richard M. Daley's commitment to developing neighborhood parks as part of the Chicago Park District. For over two generations the people of Chinatown had not had sufficient open space or outdoor recreational facilities. When the Chicago and Western Indiana Railroad closed the rail yard, the Chicago Park District acquired the land, envisioning the possibilities of even a small site with spectacular river views. At this writing the park is about five acres, but an additional seven acres, north of Eighteenth Street, will be developed in the near future.

15 Henry B. Clarke House and Women's Park and Gardens

1855 South Indiana Avenue

Open Wednesdays through Sundays. Admission $10, Wednesdays free.

The Greek Revival/Federalist style of Clarke House—Chicago's oldest house, built around 1836—inspired the organization that watches over the building to hire a landscape architect to create an appropriate period garden on the surrounding land, now called the Women's Garden and Park.

Michele McKay's design complements the symmetry of the architecture on the west side of the site (fig. 18). For this section, she specified flowers and herbs found in a horticultural manual of the period. On the other three sides, a path of mottled concrete imprinted with small leaf shapes winds around the block-deep central lawn.

Hydrangeas, sumac, black-eyed Susans, and daylilies planted within groves of cottonwood tree faithfully evoke a garden on the edge of the prairie in the early nineteenth century. A charming playhouse, a miniature duplicate of Clarke House, sits to the south. Several other elements are also present: a summerhouse, an orchard, and a walled garden. The brick fountain is by architect Tannys Langdon. H. H. Richardson's landmark Glessner House is at 1800 South Prairie Avenue, and its courtyard wall acts as an enclosing element on the north end.

FIG. 18. Clarke House, Chicago's oldest house, is now set in the spacious garden it might have had in 1836 when it was built.

PART II

NEAR NORTHEAST

Public-Private Cooperation Par Excellence

Walking downhill from Randolph Street to the lake, visitors may take a path that winds through new parkland (reclaimed during the straightening of Lake Shore Drive) to a view of Chicago Harbor. Breakwaters, sluice gates, locks, lighthouses, buoys, beaches, grassy lawns, piers, various marine structures, a Coast Guard station, and the "controlling works" together make lively patterns on the dark blue waters.

The controlling works are a crucial part of the marine engineering management here—regulating the place where the waters of the Chicago River meet the waters of Lake Michigan. Although they look like the overscaled sculptures of Claes Oldenburg and Coosje van Bruggen, these are real faucets that work. Related mechanisms open and close sluice gates for the lock through which boats must pass in traveling from the lake to the river, or from the river to the lake.

The main problem is that the level of water in Lake Michigan varies radically—certainly from year to year and some-times from day to day. Furthermore, what happens in Chicago Harbor can affect not only the city and all the communities downstream, but all of the other Great Lakes states as well.

When Chicago reversed the flow of the river in 1900, to carry sewage away to the south instead of dumping it into Lake Michigan, from which it draws its drinking water, the outflow from Lake Michigan threatened the potential capacity of hydro-electric plants to the north and east, even as far away as Niagara. (Every Great Lake except Lake Superior is downstream from Lake Michigan.) Industrial pollution, a growing urban population, and lawsuits filed by other states to stop this diversion produced the need for the elaborate structures controlling the Chicago Harbor.[33] The logic of the marine engineer rules the shapes of these structures, and they do have a certain charm.

HANCOCK BUILDING PLAZA

This charming, trellised walkway under Lake Shore Drive accomplishes several things at once: it turns what was once a garbage-strewn wasteland into a public esplanade; it offers a pictorial history of the relationship of the Chicago River to Chicago's history; and it makes this area more accessible and more amenable to recreation (fig. 19). Providing a link between Grant Park, downtown Chicago, and Navy Pier, it is a part of the city's effort to restore and make the most of its waterways.

The lighthouse-like entry gates, by architects Skidmore, Owings & Merrill (2002), frame a view of the green lawn beyond, inviting the visitor to stroll beneath its well-lit blue arches. The murals on the side walls, by artist Ellen Lanyon, are a pictorial history of Chicago. Lanyon managed to represent the evolution of the city's landscape and architecture, along with plants, wildlife, and even bridge designs in the images she painted on twelve-inch-square tiles and then fired. Text in black and white at the bottom adds informative commentary.

From the pedestrian path over the river, or from the sidewalk bicycle path on the lower level of Lake Shore Drive, you can see a barren patch of land in the east, a site of the future DuSable Park, but you cannot yet enter the space. Named after Jean Baptiste Pointe DuSable, a man of African and French descent, who was Chicago's first nonnative settler, the site has been contaminated by radioactive thorium (used in excavations for nearby constructions), and the seawall that separates the land from the water needs costly repairs.

In December 2004 a contract was awarded to the civil engineering firm Kudrna & Associates to survey the site and develop plans for its future. The following April 29, its proposal was announced in the *Chicago Tribune*. Key features include a lakeside lawn, a boardwalk, an outdoor classroom, and a "Founders Plaza," which will honor DuSable. A wetland area will re-create a vision of how the river met the lake in the days DuSable operated his fur trading post nearby.

FIG. 19. On one side the basket arches of the Riverwalk Gateway open to new parkland and Lake Michigan; on the other side they frame a view of the city. Murals lining the walkway depict the history of Chicago.

17 Navy Pier

Grand Avenue and Streeter Drive

Navy Pier has undergone many metamorphoses. In the 1916 design by architect Charles Sumner Frost, it supported three thousand linear feet of storage sheds and docks on either side of a long rectangular "land access court" for trucks, plus a streetcar line on which people could travel to a twin-towered recreational building at the east end. During World War II the United States Navy commandeered the entire space for use as a training center. From 1946 to 1965 it was home to the University of Illinois at Chicago campus. After the university moved the site lay dormant until 1976 when the City of Chicago began an extensive public-private renewal program, under the aegis of city architect Jerome R. Butler Jr., that transformed the whole area again.

Today Navy Pier is a lively entertainment and cultural center. The old head house has been recast as an exhibition hall. The land access court, now covered, contains shops, restaurants, galleries, theaters, a children's museum and a winter garden designed by landscape architect Dan Kiley. The moving spokes of the pier's iconic Ferris wheel symbolize the constant activity at the pier, and

its nighttime illumination vies with fireworks in adding sparkle to the sky after dark.

Streeter Drive curves through Gateway Park, Kiley's entrance garden at the approach to the Pier. A berm planted with tall dawn redwood trees separates the complex from the Lake Point Towers apartments to the west. Below is a spacious plaza, where water cascades from a fountain into a catch basin that also catches dozens of children at play on hot summer afternoons. To the sides are semicircular lawns planted with small-leaved linden trees. The ensemble is just right in scale, urbanity, and mood for Navy Pier, a vivacious ambience that is echoed in different form in Kiley's winter garden, a few yards to the east, inside the pier building.

Using a lofty greenhouse for a new purpose, Kiley has created not a refuge from city life but a place for a different kind of city life—a tropical paradise for grown-ups, featuring palm trees more than thirty feet high, dozens of places to sit, and countless water arches (fig. 20). Chicago is rich in fountains, and it seems each one has a different mood. Here the fun comes from sticking your fingers in the water to alter its curve and enhance the ambiance. The mood is sparkling. It is no surprise the place is often used for weddings.

The south edge of Navy pier is lined with a double row of trees to encourage promenades on Sunday afternoons. Entrances to the Chicago Shakespeare Theater, Chicago Children's Museum, Smith Museum of Stained Glass, Imax Theater, and Skyline Stage, and the staging area for the Chicago Architecture Foundation's boat tours of the Chicago River are also here. Music, dancing, weddings, museums, theaters—the place is a prime example of the new culture-producing urban nature in Chicago.

For more contemplative activities, like reading a good book, three quiet, linked parks beckon from just north of the pier.

FIG. 20. Dan Kiley created a year-round pleasure garden in the Crystal Garden at Navy Pier. Exotic palm trees and lavish fountains join to create a happy setting for weddings and other celebrations.

Jane Addams Memorial Park
550 East Grand Avenue

Just north of Grand Avenue and Lake Point Towers, in the center of a small grove of trees, stands a magnificent linden tree, appropriately marking the entrance to Jane Addams Memorial Park. Addams, a Nobel Peace laureate, founded Hull House, the first settlement house in North America, on South Halsted Street. It served as the base for her efforts to provide better living conditions for the poor and to bring them greater opportunities in art, music, and theater. Addams also championed such social reforms as the establishment of juvenile courts, justice for immigrants and blacks, workers' rights, and women's suffrage.

The path leading to Milton Lee Olive Park continues along a birch grove, through a pergola and nature trail. An adjacent wet prairie is a sanctuary for many different species of birds. Identifying signs around the surrounding fences remind us that Chicago has a remarkably diverse bird population. You can see more birds in Chicago's urban parks than in suburban, downstate, and rural Illinois combined (see Magic Hedge, in entry 46).

Milton Lee Olive Park
500 North Lake Shore Drive

The entrance to Milton Lee Olive Park begins with a wide allée of honey locusts. This leafy promenade opens at intervals to frame views of the city across the water to the north. As if a denouement were in order in this sequence, five fountains in the aerating pools of the James Jardine Water Purification Plant appear nearby (fig. 21). The grassy lawns now seem to have another function: they provide a moment of tranquility and the foreground for an expansive view of Navy Pier and its Ferris wheel. Finally, the meeting of lake and sky on the horizon is the climax in the east.

FIG. 21. A 1980s aerial view shows the infrastructure surrounding Navy Pier. Milton Lee Olive Park is in the center, just north of Lake Point Tower and west of the extensive water filtration plant, whose fountains are now part of the visual pleasure of a promenade leading to the Ohio Street Beach.

Ohio Street Beach

A sweeping view of the apartment buildings along North Lake Shore Drive, stretching north for miles, is just as enchanting at dusk in the winter when the lights go on early as it is on a summer afternoon with swimmers in the foreground. Add the blossoms on the trees in spring and the colorful fall foliage, and the place gives year-round pleasures—provided the wind is not too icy!

19 Ogden Park Plaza

Southeast corner of Columbus Drive and Illinois Street

Mandating a garden on the roof of every new public parking garage is one of the best planning ideas since the beginning of the automobile age. The motif now runs through Chicago like a recurring riff in a jazz band. This garden, part of the overall Cityfront Center master plan by architects Lohan Caprile Goettsch (entry 25), is a small but elegant example (fig. 22). The tall, broad expanse of the Sheraton Chicago Hotel to the south acts like a protective cliff, and the garden in turn softens the hotel's hard contours and provides an oasis for travelers and passersby.

Three terraces descend from the top. The highest, near the hotel, and the lowest, near the street are each treated architectonically, with the trees planted in large square beds. The middle level was originally given over to a large circular clock, a sculpture by Vito Acconci (1989) embedded in the paving materials. This clock became a favorite for skateboarders, however, and will be removed.

Entering the middle terrace now, we are drawn toward a wooden pergola covered with vines. It unifies the two separate wall gardens on the east and west, which in turn gently enclose the space. The vegetation, specified by landscape architects Jacobs/Ryan, includes iris and other water-loving plants that blossom in spring, summer, and fall. The stone planters around each tree double as intimate places to sit. At night, small light fixtures at bench level charm like miniature street lamps and also define the barriers that protect the trees.

FIG. 22. The buildings surrounding Ogden Park Plaza act as a screen for the charming garden just off Fairbanks Court. The grid design ties the plaza to the city streets, while the terraces unite it with the hotel "cliff" to the south. Trees and flowers soften the noise and refresh the spirit.

North Michigan Avenue at Chicago Avenue

Taking advantage of a slight bend in the Magnificent Mile, the Water Tower and its surrounding park give North Michigan Avenue a focal point—an anchor and a climax, a beginning and an end—a sense of place and a sense of history (fig. 23).

Erected in 1869 by architect W. W. Boyington, the Water Tower was one of the few buildings to survive the Chicago fire of 1871. Its crenellated Gothic Revival style has earned it the nickname "the old chess piece." The trees in the surrounding park have long since grown to luxuriant maturity. Newly defined geometric beds bordered with trimmed boxwood hedges are filled with closely planted white tulips in the spring and white begonias in the summer. (The design, initiated by photographer Victor Skrebneski, was executed by BauerLatoza Studio in 1999.) Period light fixtures turn on at twilight, and during the warm months the city provides movable chairs.

With this recent redesign of the park , the octagonal tower of glowing yellow Joliet limestone now seems like a charming garden folly—rather than seeming dwarfed by the much taller surrounding buildings, it appears toylike. Restricting the planting materials to a palette of dark green and white strikes a properly urbane note in keeping with the spirit of the Magnificent Mile.

The 154-foot-high tower was originally erected to house a 138-foot standpipe, three feet in diameter, which was needed to equalize pressure in the mains of the Pumping Station to the east. Although the standpipe is gone, the original staircase is intact. The space in the lower story is now a city-run gallery devoted to photo exhibitions on Chicago topics. In 2001, for example, there was a display of images from Julia Sniderman Bachrach's book *The City in a Garden: A Photographic History of Chicago's Parks.*

The Pumping Station, across Michigan Avenue, still provides 250 million gallons of water per day to the central district of the city and is worth a visit. Spectators may view the four-story interior from a surrounding gallery and examine several old pumping engines—"Old Sally,"

"Old De Paul," and "Old Pouliot." It also houses a visitor center, offering city maps and guides in numerous languages; a year-round café, with sidewalk tables in the summer; a Hot Tix outlet, selling discounted tickets for theatrical performances; and the home stage of Looking Glass Theatre, which in addition to performances offers adult classes in acting, circus arts, and ballroom dancing and runs a summer camp for children.

The Water Tower and Pumping House/Visitor Center exemplify the merger of culture-producing green spaces with public spaces as the city continues to enhance its reputation as "Global Chicago."

FIG. 23. Culture, infrastructure, and landscaping merge in Chicago's Water Tower and Pumping Station. A gallery at the base of the tower presents exhibitions. In addition to its working pumps, the Pumping Station houses a theater and a visitor center.

21 Fourth Presbyterian Church and Court
126 East Chestnut Street

Close to the heart of North Michigan Avenue, in the midst of its shopping and business district, the cloistered courtyard, or garth, of the Fourth Presbyterian Church offers a respite from the busy world of the street. Bells sound on the hour, reminiscent of medieval English cathedral towns. The chirping of birds mingles with the sounds of Michigan Avenue traffic, an interplay of vitality and tranquility that exemplifies urban nature.

The complex is the work of two distinguished architects: the church by Ralph Adams Cram and the parish house by Howard Van Doren Shaw, both designed in the early decades of the twentieth century. The broad green lawn, with new plantings by contemporary landscape architect Michele McKay, invites visitors to come in and enjoy the spread of trees, evergreens, and ornamental plants. Yews, hawthorns, viburnums, lady's mantle, lilies, lambs' ears, boxwood, wild roses, peonies, and ivy all recall the medieval associations of certain plants with religious virtues and Christian saints (fig. 24). A fountain freshens the air and beguiles the ear. All four surrounding walls are covered with ivy, making a garden so "ecologically attractive" that rabbits cavort and even an owl has been spotted in the garth.

Noontime concerts, vespers, Lenten services, lectures, and other events attract people for rest, sensory pleasure, and religious and cultural enrichment. The natural setting enhances the religious and cultural experiences, and they in turn increase the pleasures of the parklike atmosphere—another example of the exponential effect of urban nature.

FIG. 24. The courtyard of the Fourth Presbyterian Church on North Michigan Avenue is a retreat but also an invitation to the services, concerts, lectures, and other cultural activities offered by the church. The natural enhances the cultural, and the cultural enhances the natural.

The three-star view from the John Hancock Observatory, a thousand feet in the air, rivals the view from the Sears Tower and provides a panorama of the buildings and green spaces that, knit together, form Chicago's urban nature. The view from the Sears Tower has the virtue of all general patterns, clear in its depiction of the whole but somewhat abstracted. The view from the Hancock is closer to the earth, more human in scale. The building, designed by Skidmore, Owings & Merrill, houses a restaurant and an observatory on the topmost floors. Look at Chicago from the Sears Tower on arrival in the city, and from the Hancock Building for a festive farewell.

Entering the Hancock observatory, one sees the "history wall," a panorama of one hundred photographs depicting highlights of Chicago's past. Audio "sky tours" are available in English, Spanish, and German, and on the Skywalk, "talking telescopes" interpret the nighttime starscape in four languages.

Since its recent award-winning renovation, by Jacobs/Ryan, the sunken plaza at the base of the building has becoming a lively gathering place (fig. 25). Ironically, some of this transformation came about in connection with security measures put in place after September 11, 2001. New safety bollards on the sides of the building sprout daffodils and pansies, and the heavy barriers intended to keep cars from ramming the building are filled with greenery and double as outdoor seating. Turning a security problem into a design opportunity is a small triumph—one that might well be emulated in other cities.

Graceful staircases lead to the café in the sunken plaza, then morph into seats and planters. Bright yellow umbrellas shade the tables and chairs, and a pleasant water wall refreshes the air and muffles the sounds of traffic. Taken together, the observatory—helping to orient visitors with telescopes, audio tours, the historical photos—and the inviting plaza constitute an important contribution to the nature-culture synthesis emerging in Chicago.

FIG. 25. The Hancock Building's sunken plaza greets passersby with a water cascade, café tables, and other places to sit, read, or watch the passing scene. It also maximizes commercial space by allowing stores on the perimeter.

23 Washington Square Park

60 West Walton Street

The three acres that became Washington Square Park have been public land since 1842, when a real estate speculator donated them to the city. For twenty years the park was no more than a lawn with trees, diagonal walks, and simple fencing. On Chicago's north side, however, this was enough to attract wealthy citizens, whose stately homes soon surrounded the area. In 1892 the monumental Newberry Library, designed by Henry Ives Cobb, went up on its northern border. In 1906 Jens Jensen created a new design for the square, with a central fountain (fig. 26). As Julia Sniderman Bachrach wrote:

> Like "Speakers' Corner" in London's Hyde Park, Washington Square, now nicknamed "Bughouse Square," became a popular spot for soap box orators. Artists, writers, political radicals and hobos pontificated, lectured, recited poetry, ranted, and raved. A group of regulars even formed "The Dill Pickle Club," devoted to free expression. For years Washington Square's orators appointed their own honorary "king." In the early twentieth century "Bughouse Square" had such a colorful reputation that tour buses included it on sightseeing routes of Chicago.[34]

Today the lofty surrounding trees provide a canopy of shade over the restored fountain, its spacious circular pool, benches for neighbors and visitors, and period lighting fixtures. In warm weather, a colorful palette fills the flower beds, a refreshing sight whether viewed from the steps of the Newberry Library or from the benches on the diagonal walkways.

FIG. 26. Today Washington Square Park is a tranquil retreat, but it once bustled with outdoor debates and soapbox orations. Enclosed by the Newberry Library and other buildings, the square still lends itself to lively talk.

24 Connors Park

Bounded by Wabash Avenue and Rush and Chestnut Streets

This small, triangular park with its fountain and pergola provides a pleasant respite for Gold Coast residents and visitors to Chicago's Rush Street entertainment center. The magnificent elm tree at its apex alone justifies a visit, and saving it was probably the reason for the park's existence. In addition, there are airy honey locusts, daylilies, vintage lampposts with hanging planters, and comfortable benches, specified in a recent refurbishing by Teng & Associates. All in all, a charming quiet spot in the midst of a busy area.

PART III

CHICAGO RIVER WALKS

From Industrial Canal to Promenade

Chicago is delineated and permeated by water—on the east Lake Michigan, on the north and west the Chicago River, on the south the Calumet River. Man-made channels, lakes, turning basins, slips, and harbors complement the natural water network. Early in the city's history, when waterways were the nation's chief transportation routes, it was the lake and the rivers that made Chicago a trade center and the major metropolis of the Midwest. But by the late nineteenth century, this advantage had become increasingly troublesome.

Sitting in his office on Michigan Avenue at the turn of the twentieth century, Daniel Burnham saw that the city regarded the lake as its backyard. Railroad tracks, train trestles, and other industrial debris filled its shores. In his greatest gift to Chicago, Burnham turned the face of the city east, giving it a formal front yard worthy of "Paris on the Lake." Although earlier planners had advanced similar schemes, Burnham saw that he could gain support for the idea by disseminating Jules Guerin's beautiful illustrations of the Plan of Chicago of 1909. This proved essential to the plan's success. The rivers in Chicago then took on the major backyard work of transporting the flotsam and jetsam of water vessels, the garbage of passing trains, and the debris of manufacturing and other heavy industry away from the central city.

This heavy use turned the rivers into toxic wastelands. A slow turnaround began in the late 1970s, however, when federal and local money invested in pollution control and other water quality improvements began to show results. Wildlife and people started returning to the river. A second boost came with the dawning of a new civic consciousness in Chicago. In the change from the industrial age to the information age, Chicago, with its great civil engineering capacity, set out to find other solutions to its disposal problems and to turn the riverfront, like the lakefront, into an urban amenity. Leading citizens knew San Antonio's Riverwalk had made the Texas city a major tourist destination. Chicagoans hoped for a similar boom here.

In 1997 the city's Department of Planning and Development began work on the Chicago River Corridor Development Plan. A team representing the government, nonprofit organizations such as Friends of the River and Open Lands, and private developers created a blueprint for the future, which it published in 1999. Comprising five major components—development, setback ordinances, environmental action, design guidelines, and capital improvement—the plan made detailed and specific recommendations. The goal was to make the river a new recreational, social, and cultural area, with increased public access. As funds have become available, this new linear, open-air public space has started to emerge.

Already you can walk for miles along the water with the sky overhead and cliffs of skyscrapers on either bank. Holding it all together is a renewed infrastructure—balustrades and staircases, and planters filled with flowers (fig. 27). Restaurants along the promenades are opening terraced outdoor dining areas. As each section is completed its success fosters enthusiasm to improve the next.

FIG. 27. A modified Ionic volute on the armrests of the Wacker Drive street furniture ties the benches to the Beaux Arts balustrade along the river.

Once an industrial area jammed with railroad tracks, warehouses, piers, and the boardwalks of Chicago's shipping industry, the north bank of the Chicago River is now a place filled with residential buildings, hotels, and retail establishments (fig. 28). An instructive example of interdisciplinary cooperation, the new riverfront represents the combined work of private developers, public agencies, and architectural and landscape firms.

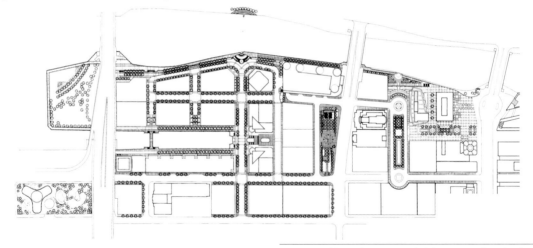

FIG. 28. Careful city planning smoothed the transition from the chaos of the city's old industrial riverbanks to the new cultural corridor called Cityfront Center.

Equitable Plaza

401 North Michigan Avenue

Starting at street level one finds a large open area that sets off the adjacent building, by architects Skidmore, Owings & Merrill and Alfred Shaw & Associates (1965). The building, in turn, gives being and definition to the plaza (fig. 29). Black marble planters and modern light fixtures with pyramidal glass tops stand in front of the building. On the north side, arched, roofless black gazebos, like modern garden follies, rise about thirty feet and surround circular pools with fountains. The pools of different shapes and fountains of different character give rise to a variety of sounds—all helping to muffle the noise from traffic on Michigan Avenue. Yews, begonias, black-eyed Susans, and birch trees adorn the sides of two long rectangular pools, each with twenty waterspouts rising in the air.

Cityfront Plaza and River Esplanade

Along the river, from Michigan Avenue to Lake Shore Drive

Initially two developers, Tishman and the Chicago Dock and Canal Trust asked Skidmore, Owings & Merrill for a conceptual plan for their properties along the Chicago River and the Ogden Slip. The goal was to integrate both

FIG. 29. As early as the 1960s the Equitable Plaza offered a unique view of Chicago's skyline, and the skyscrapers in turn gave definition to the plaza's space. The fountain is gone, but the space remains active with exhibitions, fairs, and other events.

residential and commercial buildings into this once desolate but central and potentially vital part of the city. Once the plan was finished, Tishman employed Skidmore, Owings & Merrill, with landscaper Joe Karr, to do the work on its area, west of Columbus Drive, while the Chicago Dock and Canal Trust hired Lohan Caprile Goetssch, which engaged Jacobs/Ryan as landscape architects, for its portion on the east side of Columbus Drive. As elsewhere, the City of Chicago required certain improvements, including a roof garden on top of every new garage.

Descending from Equitable Plaza to the concourse level, the visitor finds Cityfront Plaza, with an outdoor café, colorful umbrellas, and a semicircular garden at the river's edge. This is the beginning of the River Esplanade. (The esplanade is marked with signs saying "Private River-walk" but also "open to the public." I presume this means that the owners believe they have the right to close it at any time.) Defined by light fixtures that recall miniature lighthouses, this pleasantly paved walkway follows the Chicago River all the way to Lake Shore Drive. Along the way, dappled light emerges from small-leafed lindens and honey locust trees, whose rectangular beds are adorned with myrtle or ivy and flowers. Abundant benches are placed throughout the concourse, and octagonal concrete planters are rimmed with seating areas. At night the scene is lit by both the lighthouse-shaped fixtures at the water's edge and by stylized mushroom-shaped fixtures in the tree beds. The light fixtures, placed at thirty-foot intervals rather than the minimum required one hundred feet, provide a soft, continuous illumination.

This walk affords spectacular views of the city, showing the mouth of the Chicago River, how it meets the Lake, the two levels of Lake Shore Drive to the east, and the Wrigley Building and other skyscrapers to the west. There are also some other delightful surprises.

Metropolitan Water Reclamation District of Greater Chicago Centennial Fountain and Water Arc

At the same time, the Metropolitan Water Reclamation District of Greater Chicago was also looking for a site to build a fountain to celebrate its centennial. The major contribution of the MWRD, originally called the Sanitary District, was the construction in 1900 of the Sanitary and Ship Canal, which reversed the flow of the Chicago River, a feat of civil engineering experts say is second only to the Panama Canal. The two-fold purpose of the canal, as its name suggests, was to move waste and raw sewage downstream instead of dumping it in Lake Michigan, the source of the city's drinking water, and to ease shipping congestion. More recently, the "Deep Tunnel," a system of tunnels and reservoirs, has been added to the system to help control flooding and maintain a cleaner water system. When the Chicago Dock and Canal Trust gave the MWRD a parcel on the river at McClurg Court, Lohan Caprile Goettsch designed the present fountain, which was erected in 1989 and named for Nicholas J. Melas, long-time president of the MWRD.

A four-star attraction of the river walk, the fountain plays from May 1 to September 30 (fig. 30). Thrilling when the water is flowing, the granite walls of the fountain remain handsome in winter when the water is turned off. As if this were not enough, in summer an arc of water 80 feet high shoots across the river to the opposite bank, 220 feet away, during the first ten minutes of every hour

(at present 10 a.m.–2 p.m. and 5 p.m.–11 p.m., except during high winds). The spectacle, worth waiting for, creates a symbolic gateway appropriate to a Great Lakes city and sparks a festive atmosphere, with much waving back and forth between passengers on tourist boats and passersby onshore.

Continuing on along the north bank, one finds occasional pieces of sculpture, such as *Chicago Rising from the Lake*, by Milton Horn (1954), on the Columbus Drive bridge embankment. Changes in pavement patterns and the perpetual parade of passersby also enliven the scene. At the end of the walk one can see the handsome United States Coast Guard station in the distance. (Riverwalk Gateway, on the corresponding stretch of the south bank is discussed in part II.)

FIG. 30. A gateway fountain springs from a north-bank cascade and arches over the Chicago River, greeting visitors traveling by boat. People on shore regularly wave to tourists on passing cruise boats—and the tourists regularly wave back.

Finished in November 2005, this riverside plaza evolved from a mere "bullet point" in the Chicago River Corridor Plan to a terraced park honoring Illinois casualties in the Vietnam war. It is one link in a chain of planned public green spaces that will transform the old industrial-commercial riverbank into a recreational-cultural amenity, a kind of second lakefront. More plazas and a connecting walkway will be built as funds become available.

Wabash Plaza was created in conjunction with the reconstruction of Wacker Drive, which entailed moving two traffic lanes a short distance southward. The original concept plan, by DLK Civic Design, included bench/flower beds at street level. The memorial below was then executed by Carol Ross Barney of Ross Barney + Jankowsky of Chicago.

A dramatic series of terraced lawns leads down to the river level, where a memorial pool with splashing jets of water marks a niche containing a plaque and a black granite beam engraved with the names of 2,930 Illinois soldiers who died or are missing in action as a result of the Vietnam war. On the other side of the plaza, the architect has made a virtue of the necessity of providing ramps for the disabled by providing a dramatic switchback that ties the plaza to the neoclassical balustrade at street level. The plaza thus transforms the balustrade along Wacker Drive into a belvedere with a river view. From the north side of the river, or the bridge, the plaza becomes an end in itself, the climax of an architectural promenade.

More than a green space, the plaza makes a contribution to the culture of the city. The bosque of trees, flowers, sculpture, water, and flags, combined with the memorial inscriptions, create an increased historical understanding of the war and of Chicagoans' service to their country.[35]

FIG. 31. Chicago's Vietnam veterans memorial on Wacker Drive sets the list of Illinois citizens who died in the war in a soothing setting.

With the exception of the stretch between LaSalle and Wells, it is possible to walk along the north side of the Chicago River from the Wrigley Building, on the west side of Michigan Avenue, to Wolf Point, where the river's North and South Branches join. A variety of structures and plazas line the route. The Wrigley Building, by Graham, Anderson, Probst & White (1919–24), has three small plazas, one of them a launching area for boats. Marina City, by Bertrand Goldberg (1964–67), has several private boat docks and a restaurant that provides a good view of the lively life on the river. The Westin River North Hotel, formerly the Hotel Nikko, has a Japanese garden designed by Kenzo Tange. The riverside walkway of the Merchandise Mart (also by Graham, Anderson, Probst & White) is lined with sculptured heads, recalling the somewhat grandiose ambition of the late 1920s, when the building was begun. Wolf Point has a splendid view of the Loop skyline, but it is a mixed blessing. The surrounding land is a lost opportunity—an ugly, trash-ridden patch with a shabby garage.

28 South Branch of the Chicago River, West Bank

Canal Street, from Lake Street to Jackson Boulevard

The bridge house at Kinzie Street, just north of the confluence of the river's branches, typifies the juxtaposition of old and new along this stretch of the river with its wooden staircase down to the river level. The huge counterweight of the old bridge, too expensive to demolish, pilings left over from the industrial age, and new residential and tourist attractions coexist happily here in a transition zone that has something of the past, the present, and the future.

The two old Butler Brothers warehouses, between Kinzie and Washington Streets, now converted to the River Center office complex, provide a good example of the adaptation of industrial buildings to the information age. In Daniel Burnham's time, the warehouses typified his vision of the west side of the river as the industrial part of the city—no café tables then!

Today, new buildings inserted east of the old warehouses, accompanied by narrow quai-side parks with benches, create an aura of refinement consonant with the communications and other white-collar jobs now centered here. A silver nautical staircase invites strollers at the Washington Street bridge to descend to the small, riverside park next to the Boeing Company's world headquarters, between Randolph and Washington Streets. Hedges line the building's foundation, and a jazzy, zig-zag lawn, appropriate to the structure's modernity and the triangular shape of the site, is adorned with trees, benches, and a floral planter on the railing. Nighttime lighting promises to attract people after hours in the future.

Riverside Plaza (formerly Daily News Plaza)

400 West Madison Street

Two classic American skyscrapers, the Daily News Building, by Holabird & Roche, and the Civic Opera House, by Graham, Anderson, Probst & White, face each other across the river between Washington and Madison Streets. Quintessentially twentieth century Chicago, these buildings epitomize the great building period of the 1920s.

The generous, well-proportioned public space in the Daily News plaza has been a proud part of Chicago's public domain for over seventy-five years (fig. 32). The truly

forward-looking urbanism of Holabird and Root gave Chicago this distinctive public plaza and still offers a striking view of the Civic Opera across the water. Sometimes compared to a throne, the Civic Opera is lavishly ornamented with musical motifs at the crown of each section.

The spaces alongside the buildings from 10 South Riverside to 120 South Riverside repeat the forms of the Daily News light fixtures, giving the river walk along this stretch a pleasant continuity. Raised planters double as places to sit. These terraces have a semiformal air, appropriate for office workers in business clothes enjoying the sun during lunch hour.

FIG. 32. Riverside Plaza, designed in the late 1920s with the setbacks typical of the period, was years ahead of its time. Not until the beginning of the next millennium did it fulfill its potential and blossom with trees, flowers, tables and chairs, and people.

PART IV

SOUTH

Educational and Cultural Arc

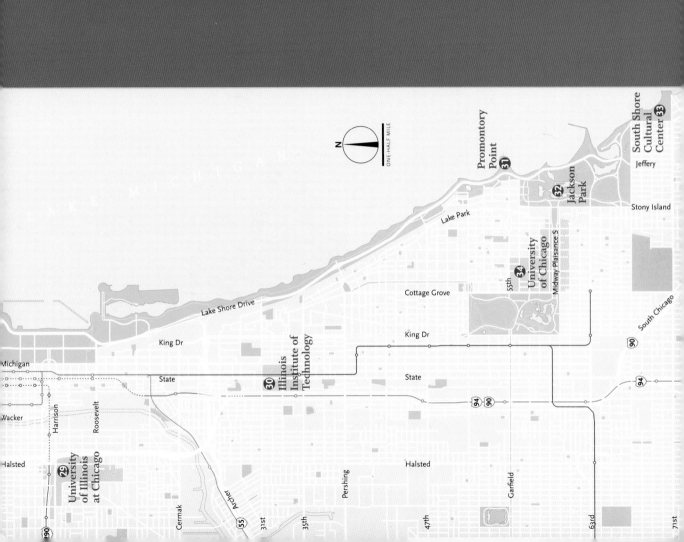

N
ONE-HALF MILE

LAKE MICHIGAN

South Shore Cultural Center **33**

Promontory Point **31**

Jackson Park **32**

Jeffery

Stony Island

Lake Park

University of Chicago **34**

Midway Plaisance S

55th

Cottage Grove

South Chicago

Lake Shore Drive

King Dr

King Dr

90

Michigan

State

State

94

Illinois Institute of Technology **30**

94 **90**

Wacker

Harrison

Roosevelt

Halsted

Halsted

University of Illinois at Chicago **29**

Pershing

Garfield

90

Cermak

Archer

31st

55

35th

47th

63rd

71st

SOUTH SHORE CULTURAL CENTER

All of the buildings on the east campus of the University of Illinois at Chicago (bounded by the Eisenhower Expressway, Roosevelt Road, and Halsted and Racine Streets) are of exposed concrete, dark brick, and tinted glass. Architect Walter Netsch of Skidmore, Owings & Merrill was responsible for the original plan, executed between 1965 and 1967.

If you look at these buildings as walls that surround green areas the overall impression is somewhat softened (fig. 33). The landscaping includes octagonal flower beds filled with daylilies, sedum, and other plants. Twenty trees flank the entrance to the dormitory at Harrison and Halsted Streets, giving it a residential air. The diagonal path from the dormitory leads to a contoured courtyard. Joined by other angled walkways, this path then leads to a large circular garden that unites the ensemble. A double allée of maple trees here graces a large lawn. In warm weather students lounge on the sloped grassy terraces throughout the court.

FIG. 33. A combination of shady trees, protective buildings, and young people stretched out on the grass give the campus of the University of Illinois a new and welcoming version of the traditional quadrangle.

At Hull House (800 South Halted Street), the one remaining building of Jane Addams famous complex, mature honey locusts and a fountain fill the oval courtyard.

In the west campus, at 1300 West Arthington Street, three-story townhouses built in the 1960s surround an interior courtyard designed by Joe Karr. Mature, tall honey locust trees shade both the lawn and the buildings. "Dorothy's Garden," a special healing garden of medicinal plants at Polk and Wood Streets, was designed by Carol JH Yetken. The sunken garden has a reflecting pool, and is supplied with annuals grown in the greenhouse of the School of Pharmacy. The firm also designed the streetscapes and sidewalk plantings along Polk and Wood Streets, at the edge of the campus. Emphasizing plants that bloom when the university is in full session in the spring and fall, the firm specified shadbush, crab apples, redbuds, and lilacs.

The south campus was designed by Wolff Clements & Associates. A new "SuperBlock" complex at the corner of Roosevelt Road and Halsted Street will have a three-thousand-seat convocation center and other features. Two green roofs, by Carol JH. Yetken, and two usable roofs are in the planning stages at this writing.[36] All in all, the new landscaping at the University of Illinois at Chicago has greatly improved the look of the campus in the last fifteen years.

Bounded by Michigan Avenue, Federal Street, and Thirty-first and Thirty-fifth Streets

Mies van der Rohe laid out the IIT "campus in a park" in a wholly modernist spirit: the solids of the buildings and voids of the landscaped areas are held together in a dynamic pattern that enlivens the space as you walk through it. Mies uses Thirty-third Street as a central axis for the symmetrically ordered campus. But playing against this traditional note is the fact that none of the surrounding courtyards are completely enclosed; instead, throughout the whole design each space flows into the next, creating a new version of the traditional university quadrangle (fig. 34). The voids are as important as the solids in shaping the experience on the ground. As you move through the grounds, these constantly changing visual relationships suggest both freedom and order—a lively expression of the Miesian ideal.[37] Significantly, Mies placed the entrances for all of the principal buildings on the courtyard sides—no building can be entered from the street. Thus these spaces are constantly enlivened by the passage of human beings during the school day.

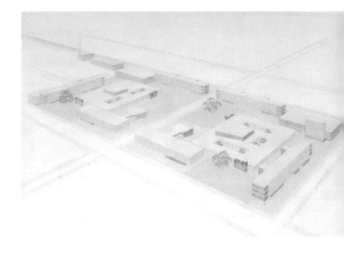

FIG. 34. Mies van der Rohe's early model of the IIT campus shows how the architect incorporated symmetry into his plan but let the buildings relate openly and freely to each other and to the surrounding landscape.

Critically important in this dynamic is the transparency of both buildings and landscaping. This succeeds due to the collaboration of Mies with his IIT colleague, landscape architect Alfred Caldwell. Caldwell understood Mies's artistic conception. Rather than obscuring the architecture with conventional plantings, Caldwell specified three principles for the campus: the design would use trees with delicate leaves, such as honey locusts, which allow the masses of the buildings to appear through the foliage; the lower branches of the trees would be cut off ("limbed up") to allow a clear view of the ground plane at eye level across the campus; and middle-level plantings, such as bushes and shrubs, would be kept at a minimum. These principles have preserved Miesian clarity at the core of the campus to this day. One especially effective example is at the south end of Siegel Hall (fig. 35).[38]

As the institution grew, new buildings rose in all directions and the campus was left without a discernible unity. State Street seemed to divide the campus into two unequal parts. In the mid-1990s Mies's grandson Dirk Lohan, a Chicago architect, developed a master plan for the campus. He suggested two major changes: building student housing between the el and State Street, and a new campus center in the block to the north, to screen the train and enclose the lawn north of Crown Hall. The landscape had also been neglected over the years, so in 1999 IIT hired Michael Van Valkenburgh Associates of Cambridge, Massachusetts, and Peter Lindsay Schaudt Landscape Architecture of Chicago to develop a West Campus Landscape Master Plan.

The landscape architects decided to transform State Street from a boundary into a unifying element. In coop-

FIG. 35. Alfred Caldwell specified honey locust trees for the IIT campus because their small leaves make the foliage semitransparent, allowing people to see the unity of landscape and buildings.

eration with the City of Chicago, on-street parking was removed, the boulevard enlarged, and the median planters from Thirtieth to Thirty-fifth Street transformed. Leafy catalpas, hybrid elms, Kentucky coffee, and ash trees now grace the walkways, providing a humane setting for students and teachers as they move from building to building. (Variety in tree selection is mandated by a City of Chicago Landscape Ordinance that prohibits using the same tree over a large area. The aim is to encourage more diversity in tree selection.) A similar treatment unites the campus from east to west along Thirty-third Street.

Thus the campus is now unified, if not transparent, on all sides. The north-south State Street corridor intersects with the east-west corridor at Thirty-third Street. Tree canopies arch over the street, making boulevards of what had been drab streets, and the boulevards, in the time-honored way, have become humane, unifying links in a kinetic fabric. The tree canopy corridor gives visitors a sense of arriving at a special place. A clear vision of the whole complex, both buildings and the lawns that connect them, is apparent at eye level. Large shade trees are limbed-up to a height of about seven feet, to permit the views to extend across the streets as well.[39] The landscape architects also designed the North Field of Crown Hall. This large open space now has sloping lawns for seating and an open center for ball games and other activities. In 2002 the Pritzker-Galvin Grove and fountain were added at the northeastern end of the field to provide an outdoor gathering place for students and faculty in good weather.

This attention to landscape has continued in relation to new construction at IIT. Peter Lindsay Schaudt also landscaped three courtyards separating the buildings that make up State Street Village, a new dormitory designed by Helmut Jahn. Each is different: one has birch trees placed naturally; another a grid of hawthorns, showing the influence of Dan Kiley; and the third bald cypresses. In 2005 this design won an Award of Honor from the American Society of Landscape Architects. The three courtyards within the new McCormick Tribune Campus Center, designed by Rem Koolhaas, have not yet been fully developed, but the building itself attends to the urban fabric, aiming to unite the IIT campus with the surrounding city. It adds diagonal pathways through the building, and envelops the el tracks in a tube that mutes the noise of the trains overhead.

Promontory Point (Burnham Park South)

Lake Michigan, at Fifty-fifth Street

Alfred Caldwell once said that he wanted his design for Promontory Point to convey "a sense of the power of nature and the power of the sea." He created a powerful sense of place, as well.

Jutting out into Lake Michigan, the peninsula has spectacular views on all sides, but it also has intimate man-made settings at every turn. Several "council rings," or low circular limestone seating areas, provide places for storytelling or cookouts (fires are permitted here), and a charming field house anchors the great lawn amid mature groves of trees (fig. 36). The beauty of Promontory Point has made it a destination for family picnics and other celebrations since its creation in the 1930s during the Works Progress Administration's extensive landfill project. Promontory Point is greatly loved, and fiercely protected, by the residents of the Hyde Park neighborhood. When the limestone pier rocks that protect the shoreline were

FIG. 36. Winter snow accents the beauty of Promontory Point, outlining the pier rocks along its edges. The L-shaped field house and tower of yellow limestone welcome cross-country skiers.

slated for removal and replacement by a concrete revet-
ment, local citizens mounted a campaign to save them. A
study by the Community Task Force for Promontory Park
showed that new limestone steps could replace the eroded
pier rocks on the peninsula's edge, and the October 4,
2005, *Chicago Tribune* reported that U.S. Senator Barack
Obama had joined the fray as mediator between the city,
the Chicago Park District, and the task force, but as of this
writing the issue remains unresolved.

Fifty-sixth Street to Sixty-seventh Street, between Lake Michigan and Stony Island Avenue

See map on pages 118–119. Park in Museum of Science and Industry garage.

Jackson Park is also the southern terminus of the historic Boulevard System (see part VII).

Jackson Park exemplifies Chicago's historic attitude toward nature. Conceived as a retreat from the stresses of urban life, it is a set-aside green space, not integrated with the streets or sidewalks.[40]

Water permeates the park. Its gentle lagoons surround open fields, and a Wooded Island, and serve as a reflecting pool for the stately formality of the Museum of Science and Industry, which anchors the park at its northern end (fig. 37). A sublime view of Lake Michigan marks its entire eastern border. Lake Shore Drive and other roads thread through the park, affording visitors easy access to any point.

The Wooded Island, created for the World's Columbian Exposition in 1893, was the site of the famous Japanese Ho-o-den pavilion. The pavilion was rehabilitated for the

FIG. 37. The lights on the isles in the lagoons south of the Museum of Science and Industry sparkle in the autumn twilight. The waters reflect the temple front and dome of the only building left from the 1893 world's fair.

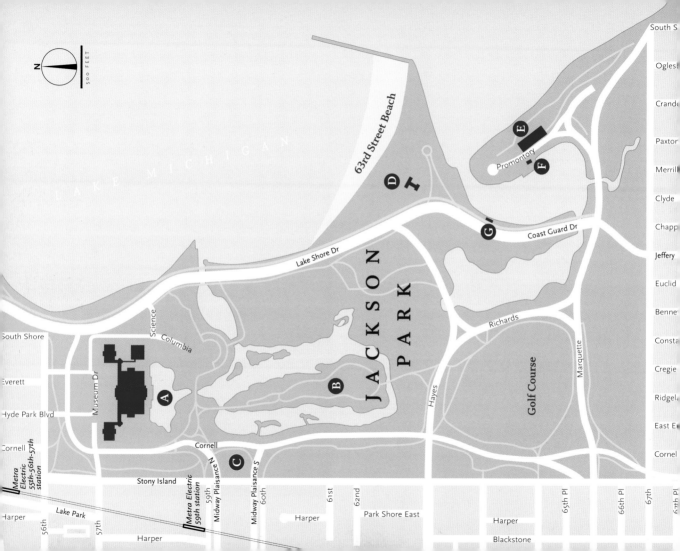

N

500 FEET

LAKE MICHIGAN

63rd Street Beach

E

Promontory

F

D

G

Coast Guard Dr

Lake Shore Dr

JACKSON PARK

Science

Columbia

Museum Dr

South Shore

Everett

Hyde Park Blvd

Cornell

Metra Electric 55th-56th-57th station

Harper

56th

Lake Park

57th

Harper

Stony Island

Cornell

Metra Electric 59th station

Midway Plaisance N

59th

A

B

C

Midway Plaisance S

60th

Harper

61st

62nd

Park Shore East

Hayes

Richards

Golf Course

Marquette

Blackstone

Harper

65th Pl

66th Pl

67th

67th Pl

South S

Oglesl

Crand

Paxtor

Merril

Clyde

Chapp

Jeffery

Euclid

Benne

Consta

Cregie

Ridgel

East E

Cornel

JACKSON PARK

A. Museum of Science and Industry
B. Wooded Island
C. Perennial Garden
D. 63rd Street Beach/Bathing Pavilion
E. La Rabida Children's Hospital
F. Jackson Park Yacht Club
G. Coast Guard station

1933 Century of Progress Exposition, and a Japanese garden, recently redesigned and renamed the Osaka Garden after one of Chicago's sister cities, still sits at the island's northeast edge. It is what the Japanese call a "finished hill–style stroll garden": mountains, lakes, and islands, represented on a small scale, are set among gentle ups and downs. Man-made elements such as bridges, lanterns, and shelters provide vistas and resting places for contemplation (fig. 38). The rich details—yellow and white water lilies floating on a water basin in the form of an open flower, the reflection of the moon bridge in the lagoon, the smell of wet pine trees, waterfalls that bring out the colors of the carefully laid rock work—induce a Zen state of mind in even the busiest visitor. The remainder of the island, to the south, has been left in a wild state as a nature sanctuary.

Getting to the Perennial Garden at Fifty-ninth Street just east of Stony Island Avenue (fig. 39) involves crossing

FIG. 38. Chicago is a world city, with many cosmopolitan touches, and one of the loveliest is the Osaka Garden in Jackson Park.

FIG. 39. The Perennial Garden in Jackson Park greets spring with bowers of crab apple blossoms that offer shade in the summer and a blaze of color in the fall.

a busy street—Olmsted's forty-foot-wide roadways, designed for "pleasure carriages," have given way to wider roads for speeding cars—but it is worth the effort. The reward is a sunken garden, bordered by limestone outcroppings, encircled by low perennials, followed by an intermediate level of forsythia bushes and flowering crab apples, with tall oak trees at the perimeter. The lawn in the center, which suggests a stage, is entered by three ramps or by gentle stairs. Designed in the 1930s by May E. McAdams, the garden has been a showcase ever since.

Sixty-third Street Beach, made from landfill, is a favored spot for swimmers and boaters. People, including many from the racially integrated neighborhoods of Hyde Park and Woodlawn, kayak, pedal boat, sail, and parasail off its shores, but the most gleeful spot is the fountain in the courtyard of the Bathing Pavilion, which delights countless children in the hot summer months (fig. 40).

Just to the south, on the other side of a channel that leads to a yacht harbor, are the grounds of LaRabida Children's Hospital, the Jackson Park Yacht Club's "Harbor Station," and a Coast Guard station. The Coast Guard station, at 6401 South Lake Shore Drive, is a white clapboard building with porches on the waterside, brick semicircular entries, gables, and the traditional widow's walk on the observation tower.

FIG. 40. Watching children play in the waters of a fountain is a summer pleasure, and the Sixty-third Street Beach House is a popular south-side attraction.

33 South Shore Cultural Center

Lake Shore Drive, between Sixty-seventh and Seventy-first Streets

Designed by architects Marshall & Fox in 1916, the South Shore Country Club's Mediterranean Revival clubhouse was a place where Marshall Field, A. Montgomery Ward, and other elite Chicagoans golfed, played tennis, and socialized. Like most such clubs at the time, South Shore did not admit African-Americans, and as the surrounding neighborhood gradually became predominately African-American, the club folded in the 1970s.

The Chicago Park District purchased the land, including the greatly deteriorated clubhouse, in 1974. Since then extensive restoration work has saved this building and its landscaped setting, which is now a cultural center not only for the neighborhood but for the larger African-American community in Chicago.

A long entrance sequence begins at the gateway, which opens to a colonnade bordering a sunken garden with a palette of blue, pink, and red flowers (fig. 41). The median strip is planted in geometric beds that draw the eye forward. Both the colonnade and the clubhouse are a warm terra-cotta color, which unifies the complex, and gives it the air of a Miami Beach luxury hotel. This ensemble is surrounded by a golf course, a park, and a swimming beach. Inside, the solarium and ballroom are frequently the setting for weddings; both are elegantly embellished with ornate moldings, ceiling decorations, and crystal chandeliers. Expansive arched windows overlook the green of the golf course and the blue of Lake Michigan beyond. The building also serves as a venue for exhibitions, concerts, and other cultural events.

The beautiful dunes setting and a nature sanctuary in the southeast part of the park add to the pleasures of this site. The Chicago Lakefront Birding Trail runs through the grounds, where many species have been sighted over the years.

FIG. 41. A formal garden graces the entrance to the South Shore Cultural Center, home to many events for the local African American community and its visitors.

Main quadrangles bounded by Ellis and University Avenues and Fifty-seventh and Fifty-ninth Streets (enter through Cobb Gate on Fifty-seventh Street)

See map on pages 126–27. Park at Sixtieth Street and Stony Island Avenue.

Today the University of Chicago has the overall air of a distinguished institution in an atmosphere of rigorous clarity and gentle humanism. This impression comes from the buildings and grounds together, the physical form of an institution that has produced seventy-three Nobel Prize winners in the world of ideas.

The historic center of the University of Chicago campus is a complex of some thirty vine-covered neo-Gothic buildings that define six spacious courtyards, or quadrangles.[41] Built in the 1890s, they enclose this four-block area without walling it off (fig. 42). Broad gateways open out on all sides, while within the atmosphere is that of a scholarly retreat. The campus has since expanded—the boundaries are now roughly Fifty-fifth Street on the north, Sixty-first Street on the south, Cottage Grove on the west, and Blackstone on the east—but the formal principles established in the quadrangles prevail to this day.

Credit for the distinction of the early buildings and grounds goes both to the designers and their clients. In the 1890s, aware of the master planning that had produced handsome new Collegiate Gothic complexes at Yale and Princeton, the university's trustees hired architect Henry Ives Cobb to design an overall plan. Mindful of the fact that their natural setting was flat, largely treeless, and somewhat swampy, and of the need to provide fresh air to ensure the health of the academic community near the industrial area of the city to the south, they also engaged gardener O. C. Simonds to design a plan for the grounds.

Simonds, noted for his work at Graceland Cemetery and in early parts of Lincoln Park, planned a picturesque setting with wandering paths and clusters of plant materials. Some of the trustees, and perhaps the architect, questioned the suitability of such an informal design for the symmetrically ordered building complex, and in 1901 they invited John C. Olmsted to come to Chicago to evaluate the site.

Olmsted submitted a thirty-six-page report the following year, arguing that Simonds' plan was "both inadequate and unsuitable" because "the buildings are many times more important than the grounds and . . . their layout and massive imposing architectural style absolutely demand, from an artistic point of view, a corresponding simplicity, formality, and dignity in the treatment of the grounds."[42] Olmsted recommended "the simplest possible geometric system, with axial vistas at either end . . . broad natural landscape effects rather than an emphasis on individual trees and shrubs." He suggested that large American elms be planted and added that "the comparative simplicity of some of the buildings, not to say the slight suggestion of clumsiness, seems to make it desirable to train vines upon the buildings."[43]

The stylistic uniformity of the buildings and their symmetrical layout in quadrangles, together with this treatment of the landscaping, gave the campus an overall coherence. The simple formality of geometric pathways also lent dignity to the surroundings. The great lawns and trees, many now over fifty feet tall, accentuate the spaciousness of the generous vine-walled setting. All in all

FIG. 42. Even a casual glance from an airplane window shows the verdure of the University of Chicago campus. The historic quadrangle and Rockefeller Chapel border the Midway Plaisance (foreground).

UNIVERSITY OF CHICAGO CAMPUS

A. Cobb Gate
B. Botany Pond
C. Hutchinson Court
D. Main Quadrangle
E. Eckhart Hall
F. Oriental Institute
G. Rockefeller Chapel
H. Graduate School of Business
I. International House
J. Masaryk Memorial
K. Midway Plaisance
L. Burton-Judson Courts
M. Laird Bell Law Quadrangle

it is this wide-open quality of the campus that gives the university its unique character. It seems the lesson of the 1893 world's fair, where generous open space had been a guiding principle, was carried over in material form to the university that is, in many ways, its spiritual heir as well as its geographical successor.

A few sections in the quadrangles are worth a lingering visit. Hutchinson Court, in the northeast courtyard, is an outdoor theater in the summer and during other seasons a sunken garden with a fountain. Nearby Botany Pond was handsomely restored by landscape architect Doug Hoerr in 2004. A handsome little bridge overlooks a water lily pool, complete with goldfish, irises, stepping stones, a circular bench, and a wide variety of plants: azaleas, pickerelweed, lily of the valley, a Japanese maple, and four bald cypresses, two in the pond, the other two on dry land (fig. 43). A glorious old ginkgo tree stands in front of the neo-Gothic cloister that seems to serve as its backdrop. Scattered lamps provide nighttime lighting. The quadrangles, harmonious and coherent, are also connected to the surrounding community by the Midway Plaisance and a revitalized Fifty-seventh Street.

The commitment of Cobb and Olmsted to the whole being greater than any single part has continued to guide the many subsequent architects and landscape architects who have worked on the campus, as well as successive presidents and trustees. Those who came after Olmsted have responded respectfully to the simplicity of his design.

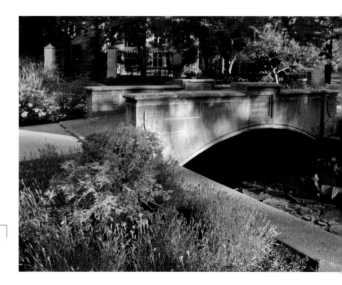

FIG. 43. Botany Pond, nestled in the northeast section of the quadrangle, is Chicago's version of a "philosopher's walk," a favorite place to stroll whether thinking about your dissertation or plans for an evening of theater at the nearby Reynolds Club.

In the next generation landscape architects Root and Hollister held to the same precepts in designing the areas around Billlings Hospital, the Divinity School, and Rockefeller Chapel.

Beatrix Farrand expressed a similar philosophy in a letter to the trustees at Oberlin College: "A campus is a place for trees and grass, northing more . . . and shrubs, but not in thickets."[44] Farrand did add a new note to the University of Chicago landscape, however, in her choice of plantings. An adherent of the Arts and Crafts movement, she believed in the use of native midwestern trees and shrubs—shadbush and crab apples—and of local stones. Another aspect of her 1929 designs for the areas around the Oriental Institute, International House, Eckhart Hall, and Burton-Judson Courts was her provision of special instructions for the final height and trimming of the vines on each individual building. Protecting the shingles, gutters, and roofs, allowing light to come in at the windows, and other aesthetic considerations all played a role in her carefully worded instructions to the gardeners.[45] She also designed benches and campaigned for plant nurseries at all the universities where she did extensive work, including Princeton and Yale.

Eero Saarinen's 1959 master plan for the Laird Bell Law Quadrangle, at 1111 East Sixtieth Street, interpreted the quadrangle concept in a modernist mode. Here the central courtyard is a reflecting pool and fountain, with small terraces adorned by sculptures by Antoine Pevsner and Kenneth Armitage.

The law school faces onto the Midway Plaisance, with its broad, sunken grassy median and mile-long vista. At each end stands a monumental sculpture: on the east Albin Polasek's *Thomas Garrigue Masaryk Memorial*, a medieval knight on horseback "rising out of fertile Bohemian soil" (1949), and on the west Lorado Taft's *Fountain of Time* (1922). The reflecting pool in front of the latter is currently being restored.

The Midway is one of several key areas restored recently, during the presidency of Hugo Sonnenschein. Other work included the Fifty-seventh Street Landscape Restoration by the Hitchcock Design Group. The new Graduate School of Business, by Rafael Vinoly, includes a south lawn and a winter garden, welcome signs of a continuing interest in incorporating landscape elements in the built environment of the university.

PART V

INDUSTRIAL CHICAGO

The enormous complex called the Port of Chicago Lake Calumet Harbor is an interconnected system of waterways and land transportation routes. It took shape in the 1870s when the United States government paid for improvements in Calumet Harbor. Sensing the enormous potential of the area for industry, the Calumet Canal and Dock Company soon followed with improvements of its own. Iron and steel manufacturing companies followed in great profusion, as did other industries, including Deering Harvester, McCormick Harvester, Gold Medal Flour, By-Products Coke Corporation, Illinois Slag and Ballast Company, and the Federal Furnace Company.

In the early days workingmen from Ireland, England, Germany, and Sweden poured into the area for the seemingly limitless job opportunities. Settling in crowded housing near the mills, the new families were in desperate need of outdoor places for recreation.

A tour of Chicago's south side, from Rainbow Beach to Pullman, provides a fascinating picture of this area, one of the world's largest industrial sites. Green spaces were inserted here and there among the various structures erected to meet the needs of the many factories and the people who worked in them. In addition, areas that were formerly toxic "brown fields" are now being reclaimed by neighborhood volunteer organizations like the Southeast Environmental Task Force; sites include the Van Vlissingen Prairie and Edens Place.

The intersections of different modes of transportation—places where railroad lines and streets meet, and where both meet water shipping routes—provide the visitor with views of turning basins, boat slips, and other water channels; iron-girder, iron-truss, link, and movable bridges; viaducts; train sheds; steel plants; and the Skyway, an elevated section of Interstate 90.

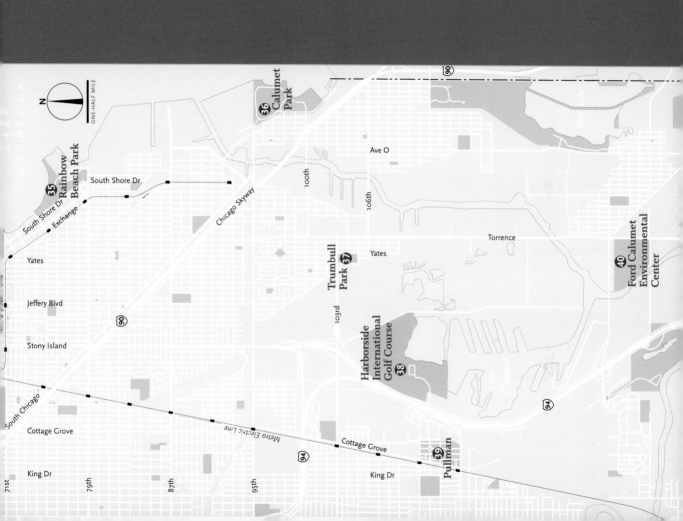

N

ONE-HALF MILE

LAKE MICHIGAN

90

36 Calumet Park

Ave O

100th

35 Rainbow Beach Park

South Shore Dr

South Shore Dr

Exchange

Chicago Skyway

106th

Torrence

Yates

37 Trumbull Park

40 Ford Calumet Environmental Center

Yates

Jeffery Blvd

90

103rd

Stony Island

Harborside International Golf Course

38

South Chicago

94

Cottage Grove

Metro Electric Line

Cottage Grove

39 Pullman

94

King Dr

King Dr

71st

79th

87th

95th

PULLMAN

35 Rainbow Beach Park

Seventy-fifth to Seventy-ninth Street, at Lake Michigan

The view of the Chicago skyline from Rainbow Beach, in the working industrial part of Chicago, is breathtaking. The sweeping curve of Lake Michigan sets off a panorama ranging from the working industrial part of Chicago to the cosmopolitan downtown it helped to spawn.

Rainbow Beach began as Rocky Ledge Beach in 1908, when a hand-laid limestone ledge was built at Seventy-ninth Street, doing double duty as a promenade and shoreline protection. In 1916 the city of Chicago acquired the land north to Seventy-fifth Street and named the expanded park after the US Army's famous Forty-second "Rainbow" Division of World War I. To provide year-round programs for the neighborhood the Chicago Park District engaged architect David Woodhouse to design the field house-beach house complex in 1999.[46]

Today the park is a favorite spot for family reunions, anniversary parties, Fourth of July celebrations, and other important occasions. Sand-colored ground-face concrete and silver-painted steel give a splashing, buoyant air to the field house, which features a terrace with airy sunshades overlooking the beach and contains a gym, offices, and activity rooms (fig. 44). Between the field house and an older beach house is a 160-foot circular lawn that brings together people, buildings, the park, and Lake Michigan. A stage for outdoor programs is nearby.

FIG. 44. Sea, sky, and sand abound at Rainbow Beach, all connected by the newly installed field house complex.

Across the harbor from Calumet Park stands the State Line Generating Station, a veritable palace of industry and the largest power generating station of the 1920s. A triumphal arch marks its entrance, and the arches in the stepped massing to the east echo the motif, suggesting the power of electricity in their reverberating forms. Here again the connection between where people lived and where they worked is made vivid. Many of the people who worked at the station, across the state line in Hammond, Indiana, lived in south Chicago. The area was also home to people who worked in the steel mills.

Calumet Park was one of several neighborhood parks erected by the Chicago Park District to fill their social and recreational needs. The field house is to this day a locus for community activities, as are the broad beach, the children's playground (designed by Olmsted Brothers in 1924), and the generous lawns shaded by mature trees (fig. 45). There are also a playing field, a large gymnasium, and smaller rooms where people with common interests can meet.

FIG. 45. The sweep of Calumet Harbor links the State Line Generating Station (upper right), houses for the people who work on Chicago's industrial south side, and Calumet Park with its field house and outdoor sports complex.

37 Trumbull Park

104th Street and Bensley Avenue

When proponents of the Reform Era in park design proposed one of their small neighborhood parks for the South Deering area it must have been most welcome. Like other parks of its era, Trumbull Park has a classically designed field house set in a landscape with playing fields and other recreational opportunities. One area is especially beautiful in the fall when the golden leaves of its long avenue of mature ginkgo trees shimmer in the sunlight (fig. 46).

The early western European immigrants to this part of the city were later followed by eastern and southern Europeans, and later still by Latin Americans and African-Americans. The surrounding area is a microcosm of industrial Chicago, built close to the waterways that were its principal arteries. Some derelict industrial structures, too expensive to tear down, still rise against the skyline. Members of the Society for Industrial Archaeology offer tours to many of these sites and hope to preserve some of them.

FIG. 46. An allée of ginkgo trees at Trumbull Park leads to a field house and other athletic facilities.

Nestled in the industrial southeast corner of Chicago, Harborside International features two eighteen-hole golf courses, two handsome Prairie School–style buildings, and a green setting created out of sanitary waste and construction rubble landfill (fig. 47). In 1996 it won the American Academy of Environmental Engineering Superior Achievement award for the ways in which it met ecological concerns. Before construction began, the entire 458-acre site had to be capped with a two-foot layer of impervious blue clay to prevent runoff and seepage of fertilizer or other chemicals into groundwater. The requirement that nothing penetrate this seal precluded the use of trees in the landscape design

The course architect, Chicagoan Dick Nugent, turned the limitations to his advantage. Inspired by the moors of Scotland, which have some ecological similarities to the prairies, he chose the "links style" for Harborside International. Such courses are usually treeless, featuring wide fairways and numerous bunkers, moguls, and water hazards, which places a premium on accuracy. Nugent first created a gently rolling topography above the absolutely flat clay cap, then added a layer of topsoil and sand as a growing medium. Bent grass is used for tees, fairways, and greens; bluegrass for the primary rough, and tall fescue for the secondary rough areas. The sloping mounds and borders are crested with dense Illinois prairie grasses, tying the golf course into the surrounding landscape. In addition, the blue waters of Lake Calumet are incorporated in the numerous water hazards.

Several engineering feats were involved in Harborside International. To obtain material for the cap, a section of Lake Calumet was dammed and drained, and two hundred thousand cubic yards of clay were removed and trucked to the site. A finger of about six acres was planted with wetlands vegetation, creating a distinct setting for the final three holes. And a drainage system was installed to trap rainwater at seven collection points and route it through the municipal sewer system back to the water reclamation plant for processing.[47] This system also prevents flooding on the golf course.

FIG. 47. The prairie grasses at Harborside International Golf Course, built on a reclaimed toxic waste site, evoke the moors of Scotland.

In Pullman you can still see one of America's first planned industrial towns (fig. 48). It may also have been the first time in American history that a landscape architect was involved from the outset in the overall design of a company town.

The 1880s were a time of bitter class conflict. Both rich and poor were frightened that the strife between the haves and the have-nots might break out into open warfare. George M. Pullman, the railroad tycoon who founded the Pullman Palace Sleeping Car Company, believed that by giving workers healthy housing in handsome surroundings he could not only foster cooperation with management and avoid labor troubles but also turn a profit. The company retained ownership of all the properties to insure rental income, and managers were instructed to effect a return of 6 percent.

To realize this scheme, Pullman hired architect Solon S. Beman and landscape architect Nathan F. Barrett to lay out a complete community. It contained a new factory to the north, a hotel, a church (which would be rented to different denominations), a market hall, a school, public buildings in a "secular Gothic" style, and housing of several kinds—generous detached houses in the Queen Anne style for executives, compact brick row houses for skilled workers and their families, and apartments or blockhouse tenements for low-wage earners. Pullman's hierarchical thinking was directly reflected in the physical environment. Class distinctions were obvious at every corner.

This experiment in social control was a disastrous failure. The resentment of Pullman's employees grew as layoffs increased and rents remained the same. Paternalistic decisions and Pullman's sermons about frugality further

FIG. 48. Pullman, once a company town, is now a tourist mecca. The hotel, church, houses, and other structures just south of the former sleeping car factory bear witness to a turning point in United States labor history.

INDUSTRIAL CHICAGO

enflamed the workers. By 1894 federal troops were encamped on the oval gardens in front of the Hotel Florence to quell the rioting. Pullman "won," over the strikers, but it was a Pyrrhic victory. He failed to prove that philanthropy based on business principles could succeed. The outcome might have been different had he made different decisions in 1893. But as it was, the experiment designed to eliminate class warfare became identified with class warfare.[48]

A glance at the map shows that the green spaces set aside in Pullman constituted only a small portion of the overall acreage. (Arcade Park was occupied by an enormous building.) The oval garden in front of the Hotel Florence was clearly ornamental, or a strolling place for wealthy guests. The green spaces around the market hall served the pragmatic end of providing easy access for buyers to meet sellers and purchase their wares. Like other cities of the time, there were no playgrounds for children, no community centers for adults, and no pools for cooling off in the hot summer months. This was landscaping before the Progressive era, when remedies to the social ills of the industrial revolution were not a high priority.

The architecture and landscape design have, however, survived this failure to accommodate new social needs and have now been reincorporated into the South Pullman Historic District. The circular garden south of the Hotel Florence is again planted in the formal beds associated with Barrett's work, as seen in early photographs. As in the 1890s, allées lead up to the site of the former market hall and broad lawns separate the factory buildings from the sidewalks and streets.

The Arcade Park Garden Club, a local group working in cooperation with the Neighborhood Gardens Project, recently added a gateway garden at 111th Street and Langley Avenue. The garden, designed by Rory Klick of the Chicago Botanic Garden, greets visitors as they enter from Interstate 94. Klick worked closely with the local garden club and specified plants from its "wish list" that she thought would be appropriate for the conditions—shrub roses and juniper, for example.

Another hidden treasure in Pullman is the cloister garden behind the Greenstone Church. Here a knot of boxwood, sweet smelling herbs, and flowers complement the building's stained-glass windows

40 Ford Calumet Environmental Center

130th Street and Torrence Avenue, southeast corner

This project is slated for completion in 2008. It is included as a convenience to future readers.

This far-south-side community, once populated largely by steelworkers, has stabilized in spite of the closure of many steel plants, thanks in part to a new Ford Motor Company plant just to the northwest corner of this site. Ford has also been a major donor to this new public-private park, developed in cooperation with other private donors and the City of Chicago's Department of Environment and Public Buildings Commission. The environmental center itself will occupy 117 acres of a 4,000-acre open space reserve of marshes, wetlands, and prairies.

In 2004 the architectural firm Studio Gang won a competition to design the center with its "bird's nest" concept. Taking nest building as its model, the firm proposed recycling salvage materials found nearby, such as slag from abandoned steel mills, to be used as concrete aggregate, and lumber from the last mill in Chicago, only a mile away from the site. Parts of the visitor center exterior will be covered with a latticelike screen made of recycled steel, which will protect birds from collisions with the glass walls and serve as an ecologically visible symbol of adaptive reuse of materials.

PART VI

NORTH

Sanctuaries and Skyscrapers

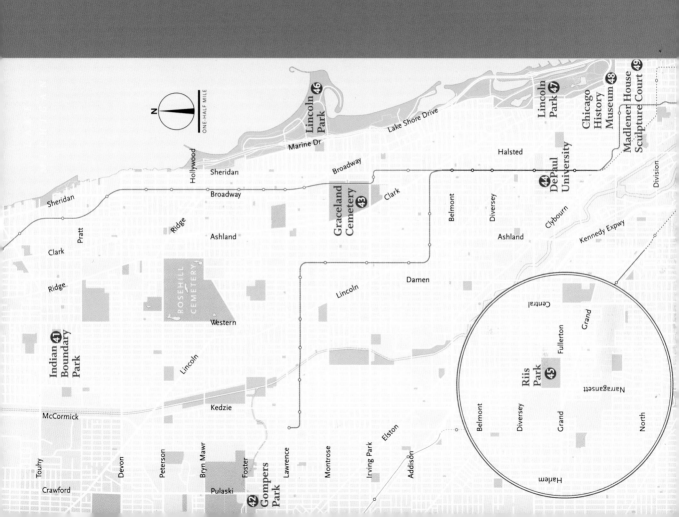

ONE-HALF MILE

N

Lincoln Park **46**

Marine Dr

Lake Shore Drive

Lincoln Park **47**

Chicago History Museum **48**

Madlener House Sculpture Court **49**

Halsted

Hollywood

Sheridan

Broadway

DePaul University **44**

Sheridan

Broadway

Pratt

Clark

Ridge

Ashland

Graceland Cemetery **43**

Clark

Belmont

Diversey

Clybourn

Division

Kennedy Expwy

Ridge

ROSEHILL CEMETERY

Western

Lincoln

Damen

Ashland

Indian Boundary Park **41**

Lincoln

Central

Grand

McCormick

Kedzie

Lincoln

Fullerton

Riis Park **45**

Narragansett

Touhy

Devon

Peterson

Bryn Mawr

Foster

Lawrence

Montrose

Irving Park

Addison

Elston

Belmont

Diversey

Grand

Harlem

North

Crawford

Pulaski

Gompers Park **42**

·LINCOLN PARK CONSERVATORY, PROPOSED RESTORATION·

41 Indian Boundary Park
Lunt and Campbell Streets

In the 1920s the eastern lawn of Indian Boundary Park and the front yards of its neighbors flowed seamlessly into each other. The plan, by architect Clarence Hatzfeld and landscape architect Richard F. Gloede, unified public and private spaces in a way perhaps inspired by Frederick Law Olmsted's work in suburban Riverside. The blending was so popular in the neighborhood that the Chicago Park District extended the idea on the northern edge of the park in the 1960s, transforming a section of Estes Street into more green space.

As part of the original scheme, Hatzfeld designed the field house at a residential scale, two and a half stories high, and in the Tudor Revival style of many of the surrounding residences. Built of brick and limestone, with a handsome slate roof, the structure's ornament recalls the site's Native American history: Indian heads in copper adorn the art deco chandeliers, a motif echoed in the relief sculptures over the fireplace.

For seventeen years, between 1816 and 1833, the territorial boundary between the Pottawatomie Indians' land and the United States ran through this section of the West Rogers Park neighborhood. Today an island in the park has been planted with prairie wildflowers—black-eyed Susans, sunflowers, big bluestem, and other indigenous grasses—in an attempt to honor the ancient history of the landscape (fig. 49). In addition, there is a small zoo, cherished by the neighbors, and all the spaces are enlivened by visitors everyday in fine weather.

The variety of motifs and layers of meaning are part of the charm of Indian Boundary Park. But the results of combining so much in one park are mixed. In a way prairie plantings in small urban parks miss the point of both the prairie and the small urban park. Prairies are quintessentially as-far-as-you-can-see places; on a small scale patches of different grasses can look ratty. One section of Estes Street, alas, comes to an abrupt halt at a stainless steel barrier, instead of gracefully joining the park. Nonetheless, Hatzfeld and Gloede's idea of a continuous flow between buildings and grounds, allowing the former to provide unity and the later variety, presents possibilities even for the present day, and is one of the reasons for including this imperfect but suggestive ensemble in this book.

FIG. 49. Layers of American history are incorporated in Indian Boundary Park, where public space merges seamlessly with private residences on the border.

Gompers Park offers an unusual microcosm of midwestern ecology. A walk beginning near the southwest corner of Foster Avenue and Pulaski Road passes a limestone circle surrounding the "origin of the stream," a bubbling creek that flows gently down to the lowest part of the thirty-nine-acre site, where it swells into a charming lagoon with wetland borders (fig. 50). This slow flowing "prairie river," whose source is in fact a municipal water pipe, eventually reaches a dam, which narrowly separates it from the park's main, natural water system, the North Branch of the Chicago River. Along the way, the path meanders through an old ox-bow of that same river.

When the Chicago River floods, the water-retentive soils hold and slowly release the water, reducing the chance of flooding downstream. Near the embankment the land rises into a dry meadow where tall-grass prairie plants abound. A grove of pines grows farther up, and on a grassy hillock above is a stand of remarkable old burr oak trees. Only slight rises in elevation make these different ecologies possible—from wetland to prairie to hardwoods in less than twelve feet.

The lagoon is the showpiece of the park. Water-loving plants fill its edges—pickerelweed, arrowhead, bulrushes. The walkways are lined with bushes bearing profuse red berries, even in November. The varied plant life also attracts a diverse population of shorebirds, herons, frogs, toads, and dragonflies. The limestone edging is inviting, in places it leads the visitor directly to the water's edge. There is a wooden bridge painted redwood red, a pier for anyone with a fishing pole, and a curved boardwalk that projects out over the water. Limestone benches offer places to rest and look at families of ducks paddling by. This remarkable section was designed in 2002 by Conservation Design Forum.

The growth of volunteer stewardship is a part of the renewal now occurring in the Chicago parks. At Gompers Park, members of the North Mayfair Improvement Association, Friends of the Chicago River, TreeKeepers, and

FIG. 50. Midwestern ecology in microcosm: a prairie river, a stream, a wetland, a meadow, and a grove of burr oak trees lie close together in Gompers Park.

EcoWatch work with the Chicago Park District's Mary Van Haaften on cleanup, weeding out invasive plants, and planting rushes, sedges, and native wetland grasses to check erosion. Together these groups have made a significant change in urban conservation.

On the north side of Foster Street is a Tudor Revival–style field house, by architect Clarence Hatzfeld, as well as other recreational facilities. The park is named in honor of Samuel Gompers, an early hero of the labor movement and longtime president of the American Federation of Labor.[49]

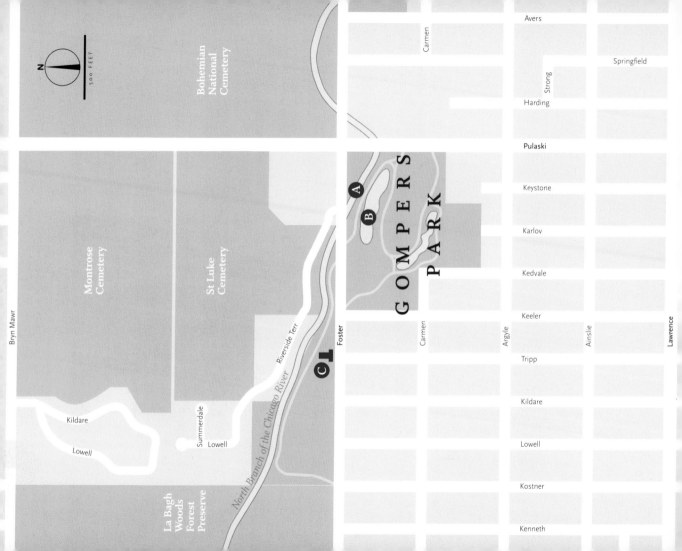

N

500 FEET

Bohemian National Cemetery

Montrose Cemetery

St Luke Cemetery

Bryn Mawr

Kildare

Lowell

La Bagh Woods Forest Preserve

North Branch of the Chicago River

Riverside Terr

Summerdale

Lowell

Foster

C

A

B

G O M P E R S

P A R K

Carmen

Strong

Avers

Springfield

Harding

Pulaski

Keystone

Karlov

Kedvale

Keeler

Carmen

Argyle

Ainslie

Lawrence

Tripp

Kildare

Lowell

Kostner

Kenneth

Gompers Park

A. River Walk
B. Lagoon
C. Field House

43 Graceland Cemetery

Clark Street, between Montrose Avenue and Irving Park Road
A useful map is available at the cemetery office.

Once one of the most renowned rural cemeteries in the United States, Graceland now offers a panorama of changing ideas about what a cemetery can be. Most Americans have changed their ideas about death since the Puritan preacher Jonathan Edwards spoke of "sinners in the hands of an angry God." In the nineteenth century, sermons—and paintings and poems—spoke of victory over death and the continuity of family life in a land of celestial bliss, but the belief had no expression in landscape art until the advent of the rural cemetery movement.

Early American rural cemeteries were inspired by Père-Lachaise, the immensely popular rural cemetery in Paris, created in 1804 in the English picturesque landscape style. In the newly industrialized nation, rural cemeteries like Mount Auburn in Cambridge, Massachusetts (1831), Green Wood in Brooklyn, New York (1838), and Spring Grove in Cincinnati, Ohio (1845) provided some of the few accessible parklike spaces for people who lived in crowded cities. Weekend revelers flocked to their lawns for picnics, family get-togethers, and other summer activities.

Inspired by these early examples, Chicagoan Swain Nelson's early plans for Graceland in the late 1860s show curving paths, gently graded topography, broad open spaces, and a small lake. Large lots were mandated in an early extension by H. W. S. Cleveland and marking off plots with railings, stone curbing, or other boundaries was prohibited. The flowing green spaces and inconspicuous low gravestones of the early period are still visible in the area south of Main Avenue just beyond the southwest entrance. The grass beneath lies like a soft green blanket over gently contoured land (fig. 51). It is easy to imagine Chicagoans of that time spreading their tablecloths here for an idyllic summer picnic. In spring, when the chestnuts spread their branches and hold aloft their blooming white candelabras, the notion that this corner of the Midwest has been trans-

FIG. 51. A panorama of historic attitudes toward interment unfolds in Graceland Cemetery. One section was designed as a Paradise Garden, with stones protruding only a few inches (lower left), while another, with closely spaced tombs, suggests a city of the dead (upper right). The latest addition is a columbarium.

formed into a celestial resting place seems to have come true.

Beginning in 1881 O. C. Simonds supervised the landscaping in Graceland for over fifty years. Early in his tenure he introduced native plants, framed vistas, outdoor rooms, and a natural style, and some of this spirit is evident today. His former partners, architects Holabird & Roche, collaborated on the design of the entrance buildings and the chapel, which were kept low, nestled into the gentle contours of the landscape.[50] Several other landscape architects also contributed, including William Saunders and William Le Baron Jenney.

In the cemetery's Edgewood section, marked by Lorado Taft's sculpture *Crusader,* the flowing, communal, natural style has been replaced by a different attitude. Victor A. Lawson, the founder of the *Chicago Daily News,* lies here, surrounded by his family. Their large site is enclosed by shrubbery, or to put it another way, the spaces are carved out of the surrounding vegetation, and the colorful blossoms create a domestic haven. This idea of privacy for each family, created by plant materials instead of fencing, appears in several other plots in Graceland.

Most striking, however, is the northern part of the cemetery, the Willowmere section. Here monumental sculpture and idyllic landscape combine in a setting resembling the Paradise Garden. Here surrounding Graceland's Lake Willowmere, Chicago's most prominent citizens lie in great tombs that, like their lakefront mansions, were designed by the leading architects of the period (fig. 52). Nearby is a majestic Ionic colonnade commemorating Potter and Bertha Palmer. At the water's edge is Howard Van Doren Shaw's tomb for the Goodman family, who founded Chicago's Goodman Theater in honor of their playwright son. Fittingly, the structure has a roof balcony overlooking the tranquil setting.

On the only islet in the lake a massive boulder marks the grave of Daniel Burnham, reminding us of his leadership in creating that milestone in the history of collaboration between architecture and landscape, the World's Columbian Exposition of 1893, with wooded island in Jackson Park (entry 32). Just to the north is the lovely Getty Tomb, by Louis Sullivan. A departure from tradition, Sullivan adorned the simple cubic volume with six rows of stars, and created delicate organic and geometric ornament for the light green copper doors.

The Ridgeland area to the west is one of the park's most historic areas. There Simonds used indigenous plants, developing a forerunner of the Prairie School. Today yarrow, columbine, and trumpet bush are planted in sections set within the great lawn.

The middle part of the cemetery is filled with the tombs of other Chicagoans with monuments of great va-

riety. One of the loveliest is the Marshall Field memorial, on Dell Avenue. Here the sculptor Daniel Chester French and the architect Henry Bacon worked together to great effect. (Ten years later they again collaborated, on the Lincoln Memorial in Washington, D.C.) Presiding over a reflecting pool is *Memory*, a statue of a seated woman As her left arm gestures toward a reflecting pool, she seems to invite you to rest on the shaded benches nearby. Small gravestones set in the ground, like little kneeling pads, mark other members of the Field family. The plot feels like a family chapel. With flowering shrubs and evergreens, the mood is one of everlasting peace.

A columbarium resembling a walled garden, with a central fountain, was added in the 1990s, creating a place for cremated remains. Designed by Wolff Clements & Associates, the red granite of the wall matches that in the Holabird & Roche chapel nearby.

Fullerton Avenue, between Halsted and Racine Streets

In a masterstroke of visionary urban planning, in the late 1980s architect Joseph Antunovich asked that university president John T. Richardson request city permission to close off one block of Seminary Avenue, between Fullerton and Belden Avenues. This change allowed the architect to give the new library he was designing a more collegial setting (fig. 53). at the edge of a traditional academic quadrangle. The symbolic value of this landscaped setting goes far beyond increased ease of circulation for faculty, students, and staff, contributing to a new sense of place and integrating the campus into the surrounding neighborhood.

FIG. 53. The power of a single architectural decision is demonstrated here. Closing one block of Seminary Avenue allowed DePaul University to create a landscaped space that, like a traditional quadrangle, unites the surrounding buildings, while also reflecting the university's urban mission.

6100 West Fullerton Avenue

In 1898 Jacob A. Riis, photojournalist, reformer, and author of the famous exposé *How the Other Half Lives*, gave a speech at Hull House in Chicago appealing for playgrounds and parks for people who live in tenements. Eighteen years later the park that honors his contribution to social reform was dedicated near the western edge of the city.

The transformation of the fifty-five-acre site was gradual, but there were promising elements from the outset. A glacial ridge provides topographic drama, and Alfred Caldwell's design took full advantage of the roughly twenty-foot change in elevation. A circular drive (no longer extant) unified the other elements: a low-lying meadow, "Crabapple Lane" to the west, a lagoon and "Grass Lane" on the south (fig. 54). West of the utility shed is a grove of old linden trees and a giant burr oak. Recently Caldwell's stone-edged lagoon and naturalistic plantings were restored by Wolff Clements.

FIG. 54. A beautiful drawing can capture the concept of a park, as Alfred Caldwell's plan for Riis Park shows. The circular drive is no longer extant, but "Crabapple Lane," the lagoon, the grove of linden trees, and a giant burr oak still stand.

Over the years other recreational elements have been added, notably a water playground in 2002. This interactive fountain is the delight of neighborhood children in the summer months and perhaps an even greater delight to the grown-ups who watch them as they clamber over a bridge suspended between gabled pavilions, slide down gigantic tubes, and turn valves that suddenly emit great arcs of water.

Lincoln Park grew from what was once a small cemetery north of North Avenue. In 1869 all but one of the graves were moved and landfill added to form a vast open area that now extends over five miles, from Oak Street Beach in the south to Ardmore Avenue in the north. Unlike Chicago's other historic parks, where the buildings and landscape scheme were coordinated, no one landscape architect designed Lincoln Park. It is a string of green spaces put together over time, a series of loosely related landscapes (fig. 55). With six bathing beaches, a golf course and driving range, three harbors, a conservatory, several cultural institutions, and countless sculptural monuments this linear park has a greater variety of facilities than any other park in Chicago. It is also the city's most heavily used park and, at 1,028 acres, its largest. At one point in the late 1980s, I found members of nineteen different ethnic groups occupying a single acre on a warm summer day. When presenting my findings, I therefore claimed that Lincoln Park had the greatest ethnic diversity of any park in Chicago. My colleague Kenneth Fidel, a sociologist, later told me I had understated my case; I should have said "in the world."[51]

The park is distinguished by the work of several notable landscape architects and architects. Among others, Swain Nelson designed the southernmost part (in 1865), Alfred Caldwell the Lily Pool, J. L. Silsbee the conservatory, and Andrew Rebori the golf shelter.

Lake Shore Drive follows the west edge of the park's northern half (the area around Montrose Avenue is discussed in this entry), then crosses over and runs along the lakefront in the southern half (the following entry deals with some of the highlights of this segment).

FIG. 55. Lincoln Park, Lake Michigan, the skyscrapers of Chicago, and the streets connecting them are woven together into an urban fabric traversed by motorists, bicyclists, and pedestrians.

L A K E   M I C H I G A N

Montrose Point

Magic Hedge

Montrose Beach

Montrose Harbor

Belmont Harbor

Lake Shore Dr

Cricket Hill

Simonds

Roscoe
Aldine
Hawthorne
Stratford
Roscoe
Brompton

Broadway

Patterson

Brompton

Elaine

Roscoe

Buckingham

Aldine

Melrose

Marine Dr

Lawrence
Lakeside
Leland
Eastwood
Wilson
Windsor
Sunnyside
Agatite
Montrose

Junior Terr
Junior Terr
Hutchinson
Gordon Terr
Bittersweet
Irving Park
Sheridan

Clarendon

Broadway

Grace
Bradley
Waveland
Addison
Reta
Cornelia
Newport
Roscoe

Dayton

N

500 FEET

LINCOLN PARK

Lake Shore Drive

Peggy Notebaert Nature Museum

Alfred Caldwell Lily Pool

Cannon

Lincoln Park Zoo

South Pond

Café Brauer

Chicago History Museum

Wabash

State

Dearborn

Clark

LaSalle

LaSalle

North Pond

Lincoln Park Conservatory

Stockton

Lincoln Park West

Commonwealth

Clark

Orleans

Lincoln Park West

Orleans

Wells

Crilly

Crilly

Wieland

North Park

Orleans

Sheridan

Pine Grove

St. James

Roslyn

Arlington

Hampden

Wrightwood

Sedgwick

Wisconsin

Hudson

Fern

Hudson

Wellington

Oakdale

Surf

Lehmann

Cleveland

Menomonee

Meyer

Briar

Barry

Broadway

Clark

Drummond

Deming

Arlington

Geneva

Kemper

Cambridge

Belden

Grant

Lincoln

Dickens

Hudson

Mohawk

Larrabee

Eugenie

Waterloo

Fullerton

Webster

Howe

Willow

Vine

North

Barry

Clark

Schubert

Wrightwood

Burling

Burling

Orchard

Concord

Weed

Halstead

Oakdale

George

Wolfram

Diversey

Dayton

Burling

Armitage

Halstead

Dayton

Dayton

A natural dune, rare in a big city, Montrose Beach has recently been placed on the Illinois Natural Areas Inventory by the state's Nature Preserves Commission. Along with typical dunes flora and fauna, the beach also contains an unusual geographical feature called a panne—a wet depression in a dune/swale system.[52]

Just south of the beach is Montrose Point, a onetime U.S. Army Nike missile site. Now called Cricket Hill, the site is popular for sledding in the winter and kite flying in the summer. A bird sanctuary known as the Magic Hedge, on a sand hill just east of Montrose Harbor Drive, is a highlight during the spring and fall migration seasons.

It might surprise some people, but Chicago attracts a greater variety of birds than all of suburban and rural Illinois combined. Birds use waterways as reference points on their flights north and south, and the stretch of grassy green between the waters of Lake Michigan and the vast sprawl of concrete to the west promises an inviting place to rest. A great number of species and individuals are regularly listed by bird-watchers at the Magic Hedge. Sparrows are there, of course, but also cuckoos, flycatchers, vireos, thrushers, warblers, tanagers, and such vagrants as reddish egrets, groove-billed ani, and Kirtland's warbler. The nearby harbor, beaches, and lake are also landing fields for loons, grebes, gulls, and other waterfowl and shore birds. Peregrine falcons have been spotted nesting nearby, and we welcome these magnificent predators, which feed on Rock Doves, better known as common city pigeons.[53]

Non–bird-watchers, children and adults, enjoy the primeval aspect of the natural environment at the Magic Hedge. Even the parking spaces along the driveway have something to offer: a spectacular view of Chicago during the day, a magical view of the harbor and city lights at night.

In the southern half of Lincoln Park—nestled between Lake Shore Drive and the lagoon on the east and the Lincoln Park neighborhood on the west—lies another string of attractions, considered here from north to south.

North Pond

Between Diversey and Fullerton Avenues

Before recent changes both the landscape and the building at North Pond were undistinguished. The terrain was a dune, filled with scrub oak and often used as a dumping ground, and the building was a small brown-brick structure that served as a warming house for skaters.

The Chicago Park District, working with Thompson Dyke & Associates as landscape consultants, replaced the patchy turf grass at the edges of the pond with rich and diverse plantings of native aquatic and upland prairie plants (fig. 56). Since then volunteers have conducted flower walks on a regular basis, helping visitors appreciate the many varied prairie specimens: little bluestem,

FIG. 56. Just a few blocks from one of the densest parts of the city, North Pond in Lincoln Park offers a place to feed the ducks, fish, loaf in the sun, or watch the clouds. The contrast enhances both the vitality of the city and the tranquility of the park.

sky-blue aster, nodding wild onion, side-oats grama, butterfly weed, purple prairie clover, rough blazing star, wild quinine, prairie phlox, coneflowers, false dragonhead, northern prairie dropseed, showy goldenrod, rattlesnake master, shooting star, and wild bergamot. Many fauna are also at home in the ten-acre site: squirrels, turtles, rabbits, opossums, and a world of butterflies and dragonflies.

Architect Nancy Warren added a large dining room to the old warming house, and installed rows of nine-foot-tall French doors on three sides of the new North Pond Restaurant. In fair weather these doors open onto a terrace, from which a view of the Chicago skyline appears across the pond and over the treetops, and on snowy days sparkling light from the restaurant enlivens the landscape. A large fieldstone fireplace, oak shelves, and pieces of copper and pottery in the Arts and Crafts style decorate the interior spaces. With its horizontal lines and low flat roof, the building exemplifies the Prairie School, which had its origins in exactly the kind of landscape and wildlife habitat now recreated here.

When Mayor Richard M. Daley and the U.S. Fish and Wildlife Service signed the Urban Conservation Treaty for Migratory Birds they selected North Pond as an appropriate signing place.

Peggy Notebaert Nature Museum
2430 North Cannon Drive

Given Montgomery Ward's lifelong battle to keep the lakefront "forever open, clear, and free" of obstructions, some Chicagoans may object to any new buildings in Lincoln Park.[54] The Notebaert Nature Museum may, however, soften their attitude. It is a sharp intrusion in the landscape, yet indoors and outdoors work together here, partly because the distinction between them is clear, and partly because the museum is placed on a narrow, otherwise unused plot of land (fig. 57).

The architects, Perkins and Will, created a design reflecting the interdependence of the natural and human-made worlds and were careful to preserve many of the surrounding trees. The mission of the museum, a new incarnation of the Chicago Academy of Sciences (CAS), is to interpret natural history, so the architects created a design reflecting the interdependence of the natural and human-made worlds. Their "pond gateway" features a limestone wall and paved paths leading to a fishing pier that has wet prairie plantings on the west. Conservation Design Forum worked with the architects in specifying the plant materials.

FIG. 57. The Peggy Notebaert Nature Museum embraces and is embraced by its surroundings. The building, emphasizing the interdependence of the manmade and the natural world, exemplifies the mission of the institution.

The CAS, Chicago's first museum, was founded in 1865 by Robert Kennicott and others who wanted to preserve some 250,000 specimens of the Midwest prairie, which they feared were already being lost to the farmer's plow. The museum has since become more than a collection of specimens. Today any one of 75 species of butterflies may light on your shoulder as you stroll through the indoor butterfly garden; over the course of a year an amateur lepidopterist can see over 250.

On the top of the building, a compact zigzag roof garden, also by Conservation Design Forum, shows the great variety of plantings—sedums, perennials, and even a small tree—that can be grown on a roof in soil and gravel coverings ranging from six inches to eighteen inches in depth. A living laboratory, the roof also gathers data, such as temperature and rainfall measurements, so that its effectiveness can be compared with other green roof systems. Interpretive panels explain that a green roof is not just a pretty rest stop for visitors, but also helps our urban environment, by reducing energy needs, absorbing rainwater, filtering pollutants, reducing smog, providing wildlife with food and water, and offering a nice view for neighbors who live in surrounding apartment buildings. A stunning view of the park and city completes the picture.

"A sanctuary of the native landscape"—Alfred Caldwell's summation in 1938 of his design concept for the Lily Pool is just as apt today. In no other public garden can people feel the magic of a nearly vanished landscape form: a pond within a midwestern wooded glade.

Handsome as the pool's Prairie School gateway is, it scarcely prepares you for the vista that opens beyond. The clear waters of the lagoon sparkle; golden light filters through the leafy canopy overhead; the reflections and shadows of the trees dapple surfaces everywhere—especially enlivening the stratified limestone of the edges, pathways, and the cascade.

In the middle distance a flat-roofed open pavilion of wood and limestone offers places for rest under its overhanging eaves (fig. 58) An ideal is realized here: the architecture and the landscape are mutually enhancing. The informal rectilinear structure gives a center to the flowing water and swaying grasses, a welcome stillness, and the moving plant materials bring freshness and variety to the architectural setting. Each stands well alone, yet their togetherness seems inevitable.

The Lily Pool is a man-made, distilled image of a part of the larger Midwest. Limestone formed when the inland seas that overlay the region receded. Here it is artfully arranged, magnifying the sense of place. The pool amid rocks recalls a later geologic time when the glacial meltwaters cut through that underlying limestone stratum. The paths surrounding the pond undulate almost imperceptibly, mimicking the gentle topography of Illinois. Trees grow in the upland area, reminding us that ecologically this is still part of the Eastern Woodlands. Around the pond native iris predominates—a good decision. When they are not in bloom their leaves provide sharp, linear architectonic notes on a small scale, giving definition to the lower elevations and providing a contrast to the curvilinear lily pads. A "council ring" on a hillock above the southeastern edge of the pond symbolizes Caldwell's debt to his mentor, Jens Jensen, the founder of the Prairie Style in landscape architecture.

Wolff Clements & Associates, who restored the Lily Pool in 2000, ordered the removal of some trees, such as

FIG. 58. Centered on a reflective lagoon, accented by limestone rock work and a handsome Prairie School pavilion, the Alfred Caldwell Lily Pool is a masterpiece of landscape design. The plantings play a secondary role to the water, the stone, and the building.

white poplar and European buckthorn, which had shaded out some of the undergrowth, and the replanting of staghorn sumac, nannyberry, and other local plants, in the spirit of Caldwell's commitment to using native materials. Recent overgrowth of some of the plants has, however, obscured the clarity of the original and should be corrected.

In spite of the overgrowth, there is an overarching unity provided by Caldwell's rock work, the pavilion, and the central water feature. Landscape architecture is not just about the vegetation! These original water and hardscape elements still dominate the garden, continuing to make it one of the nation's most significant works of art, and as such should be the focus of future preservation efforts. Its 2006 designation as a National Historic Landmark should ensure that it receives the level of maintenance it deserves.

Lincoln Park Conservatory

Stockton Drive and Fullerton Avenue

The conifer garden on the northwest side of J. L. Silsbee's 1894 conservatory is a small jewel at the heart of Lincoln Park. Some of the conifers are rare, and all are thriving near the gnarled branches of three ancient crab apple trees. Grassy, curving pathways lead past rows of hosta and irises. Intimate in scale, the shaded space is calm and lovely—the result of Chicago Park District gardeners doing their careful work year after year. These heroes of our green spaces deserve to have their praises sung more often.

The conservatory itself, its glass domes billowing like giant soap bubbles (fig. 59), encloses four separate areas: the Palm House, the Fernery, the Orchid House, and the Show House. Among the many attractions are a fifty-foot-tall fiddle-leaf rubber tree and a collection of cycads, ancient species from the time of the dinosaurs. The plaques tell us that Illinois was once a wet tropical forest where a small dinosaur would have felt at home.

FIG. 59. The Lincoln Park Conservatory, with its billowing roofs, is an airy background in summer and a lush retreat in the cold winter months. This illustration shows the conservatory after a proposed restoration.

To the south of the building is a formal garden, with a sculpture, a fountain, and an ever-changing assortment of annuals, and across Stockton Drive the informal Grandmother's Garden, also known as the Old English Garden. The combination recalls the juxtaposition of Beaux Arts layout and informal landscape at Chicago's 1893 world's fair. Also to the south, in the Lincoln Park Zoo, is the new Pritzker Family Children's Zoo, which features exemplary landscaping.

Café Brauer and South Pond

2021 North Stockton Drive

A masterpiece of Prairie School architecture, Café Brauer, designed in 1908 by Dwight H. Perkins, is handsomely sited on South Pond in Lincoln Park (fig. 60). To quote landscape historian William W. Tippens:

> The massing includes a large closed central pavilion flanked by two graciously curving loggias. A broad expanse of green tile roof with deep overhangs, combined with earthy red brick, subtle terra-cotta details, and polychromatic mortar,

settles the building into the landscape. Viewed from Stockton Dr. to the west, the large block of the central pavilion dominates, while the curving loggias recede. But on the lagoon side the two loggias are seen to wrap around the end of the pond. Simultaneously the loggias contain the water, and the lagoon's form controls their curves. . . . From the loggias, which open off the Great Hall, the skyline unfolds to the south.[55]

One of the charms of the scene at South Pond is the reflection of the café in the water. Adding to the vivacity are families in swan boats and paddleboats sharing the pond with ducks and geese.

Recent efforts by the Chicago Park District have helped to reestablish indigenous plantings along the shore and have encouraged nesting of waterfowl in the wet prairie area and the return of butterflies to the slightly higher and drier beds. Friends of Lincoln Park, a citizen's watchdog group, worked carefully with the Chicago Park District in the restoration of Café Brauer—one of the triumphs of public-private cooperation and volunteerism in Chicago.

FIG. 60. Nestled in the landscape, the loggias of the Café Brauer are open to the pleasures of boating, fishing, or dining in Lincoln Park.

48 Chicago History Museum

North Avenue at Clark Street

The eastern elevation of the Chicago History Museum, combined with the walkways curving through its lawn and gardens, best shows architects Graham, Anderson, Probst & White's intention of integrating the building with its host, Lincoln Park (fig. 61). The east entrance, facing Lake Michigan—Chicago's front yard—was originally the museum's front door. Here steps of the Georgian-style building rise to the grand second floor, the *piano nobile*, which originally contained the chief ceremonial and exhibition spaces of the museum. These steps and the temple front porch are also the stage, and the expansive lawn the seating area, for one of Chicago's most treasured traditions, the annual recitation of the Declaration of Independence on the Fourth of July.

Currently the building is undergoing a renovation. According to museum president Gary Johnson, the new space on the east side will follow the Georgian-style architecture of the 1932 building, with eight windows offering views of the Uihlein Plaza, Lincoln Park, and Chicago's Gold Coast. Architects Hammond Beeby Rupert Ainge have also incorporated the original lobby and extended it to the north and south to create a large reception area adjacent to the terrace. Moving this space for special events to the eastern part of the building will, it is hoped, encourage attendees to interact more with the park as they enter and leave.[56]

A notable statue of Abraham Lincoln by Augustus Saint-Gaudens, with a based designed by architect Stanford White, stands a few yards to the east on North Avenue. It has recently been given a suitable approach allée by Friends of Lincoln Park.

FIG. 61. In a new remodeling, the classical eastern facade of the Chicago History Museum will regain its focus as a center for special events, such as the reading of the Declaration of Independence every Fourth of July.

49 Madlener House (Graham Foundation) Sculpture Court

4 West Burton Place

Open by appointment only. Call 312-787-4071.

The overhanging crab apple tree and its leafy shadows in this sculpture courtyard, designed in 1986 by John Vinci and Philip Hamp, are perfectly in tune with the architectural fragments by Louis Sullivan and others that surround it (fig. 62). The objects—all donated to the Graham Foundation—include many with botanical motifs: a sandstone mullion cap decorated with a stylized acanthus leaf, a cast-iron cornice panel with geometrized leaves and flowers, a limestone impost block that turns into elegant foliage, a terra-cotta column with Prairie School ornament, and a large acroterion on a corner block.[57] A pamphlet available at the garden states:

Although there was no initial intention to focus the collection on Sullivan, it is interesting now to see how well it encapsulates his brilliant but tragic career. Virtually every piece presently exhibited reflects some aspect of Sullivan—work of his mentor, John Edelmann, and his . . . most gifted disciples, Frank Lloyd Wright and George Grant Elmslie, . . . [and] Hugh Garden. . . . Finally, in counterpoint to Sullivan, are the pieces from the Field Museum and Tribune Tower, buildings despised by Sullivan, but representative of Chicago's rich architectural heritage.

Thanks to careful placement of the many fragments, the walled garden retains an airy atmosphere. Hostas at ground level soften the paving stones, and two ginkgo trees flank the staircase into the house. Madlener House was designed by Hugh M. G. Garden in 1902 when he worked for Richard E. Schmidt.

FIG. 62. A small space, the courtyard of the Graham Foundation's Madlener House is a treasure trove of Chicago's historic architectural sculpture.

PART VII

WEST CHICAGO'S "COUNTRY CLUBS FOR THE POOR" AND THE HISTORIC BOULEVARD SYSTEM

Two systems of landscape urbanism are woven together on the west side of Chicago, the Boulevard System and the West Parks. This section also describes some noteworthy west-side sites that are not directly linked to the Boulevard System.

Introduction to the Boulevard System

The heart of Chicago is surrounded by a remarkable urban amenity—a necklace of wide green boulevards and interconnected parks, its famous Boulevard System. At the turn of the twentieth century you could take a carriage ride (and today you can still drive, bike, or walk) for twenty-eight miles around the center of the city, nearly always in or on the edge of a leafy open space. It all started when the Illinois legislature passed the Chicago Parks bill in 1869, outlining parks all over the city, linked by miles of landscaped boulevards. Although many landscape architects worked in the various parks, the system works as a unit, as the designers working separately for the South, West, and North Park Commissions had a common goal.

The boulevards, many of them 250 feet wide, with generous trees and floral plantings, still connect nine of the city's historic parks and for long stretches are bordered by handsome residential architecture. In his insightful chapter on the Chicago parks in *Constructing Chicago,* Daniel Bluestone quotes an editorial in the *Chicago Tribune* of 1873 :

Anyone familiar with the country who visited the parks could scarcely deny that Nature commends itself more with modern improvements than it does without them. . . . The advantages of improved Nature are obvious. A Saturday in Lincoln Park alone is sufficient to establish its superiority over wild and uncultivated Nature. You have hills which are not too high to climb, sheets of water whereon your boats may float with the security, if not the grace, of a swan; banks to recline on without being haunted by the terror of snakes or black bugs; good roads to drive on that are never dusty or too muddy; rustic bridges to cross without the danger of breaking through . . . pretty women, equipages, and the greeting of friends to

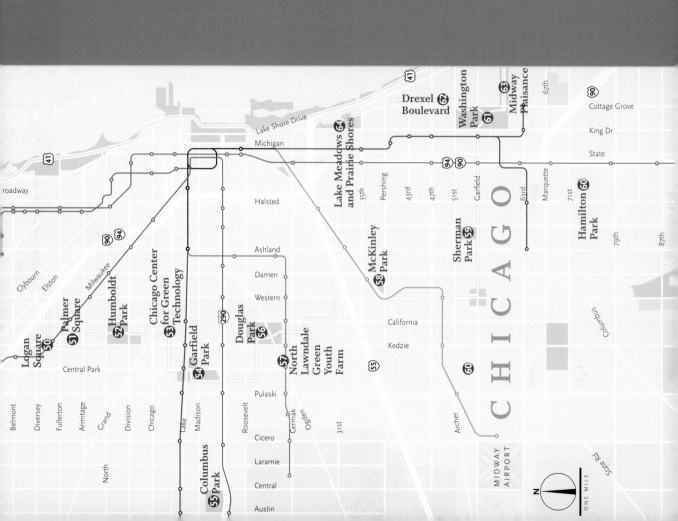

LAKE MICHIGAN

Lake Shore Drive

Michigan

Halsted

Ashland

Damen

Western

California

Kedzie

Roosevelt

Cermak
Ogden

31st

Archer

roadway

Clyburn
Elston

Milwaukee

Belmont

Diversey

Fullerton

Armitage

Grand

Division

Chicago

North

Central Park

Pulaski

Cicero

Laramie

Central

Austin

Drexel
Boulevard

Washington
Park

Midway
Plaisance

67th

Cottage Grove

King Dr

State

Marquette

71st

79th

87th

Columbus

Lake Meadows
and Prairie Shores

35th

Pershing

43rd

47th

51st

Garfield

63rd

McKinley
Park

Sherman Park

Hamilton
Park

CHICAGO

Logan
Square

Palmer
Square

Humboldt
Park

Chicago Center
for Green
Technology

Garfield
Park

Douglas
Park

North
Lawndale
Green Youth
Farm

Columbus
Park

MIDWAY AIRPORT

State Rd

ONE MILE

N

50 Logan Square
51 Palmer Square
52 Humboldt Park
53 Chicago Center for Green Technology
54 Garfield Park
55 Columbus Park
56 Douglas Park
57 North Lawndale Green Youth Farm
58 McKinley Park
59 Sherman Park
60
61 Washington Park
62 Drexel Boulevard
63 Midway Plaisance
64 Lake Meadows and Prairie Shores
90 Hamilton Park

GARFIELD PARK CONSERVATORY

enliven the scene, picturesque views that are panoramic in the constant changes the people make: the delusion of bucolic pleasures without the stern reality of bucolic fatigue, monotony and stupidity.[58]

Even in its early days, Chicagoans looked at parks not just as an escape, or "a way of getting away from the world, but as a way of getting the world to come to Chicago."[59] Then, as now, its green spaces were among the great cultural attractions of the city.

A number of historic events contributed to the development of this boulevard system.

- *The vision of Chicago real estate man John S. Wright.* During the 1840s Chicago developers had created a number of public squares to bolster the economic value of their properties—including Washington Square (entry 23), but by 1849 Wright saw that these amenities could be put together on a larger scale and benefit the whole city. Wright may have been the first to envision a parks and boulevards system such as soon graced Paris, Boston, Washington, D.C., and many other cities.

   I foresee a time, not very distant, when Chicago will need for its fast increasing population a park or parks in each division. Of these parks I have a vision. They are improved and connected with a wide avenue, extending to and along the lake shore on the north and the south, and surrounding the city with a magnificent chain of parks and parkways that have not their equal in the world.[60]

- *The Parisian influence.* In the 1850s Georges- Eugène Haussmann, prefect of the Seine in Napoleon III's era, redesigned Paris making it a fittingly magnificent capital for imperial France, with long, tree-lined boulevards, and splendid parks. Returning home from their European grand tours, influential Chicagoans wanted to emulate the Champs-Elysées and the Bois de Boulogne. European influence also came via Frederick Law Olmsted, William Le Baron Jenney, and H. W. S. Cleveland. These three designers, all active in Chicago in the late 1860s, knew Paris well, and all must have seen the Avenue de l'Imparatrice between the Bois de Boulogne and Paris, which was planted informally, in a parklike fashion. It is difficult to say which of them first designed Chicago's boulevard system. Olmsted's other work of the time—Riverside, Illinois, and the Eastern Parkway leading into Prospect Park in Brooklyn—are manifestations of this same influence.[61] The idea of connecting parkways or boulevards was like a new pollen in the atmosphere—it spread everywhere among enlightened people who wanted to bring the civilizing influences of parks to their cities. By the late 1860s it was a shared vision in Chicago.

- *Empowered park districts*. Enlightened Illinois legislators passed enabling legislation in 1869, giving Chicago's three extant park districts—South, West, and North—power to regulate land use within four hundred feet of the boulevards and to establish setbacks of fifty feet. (Development along Diversey Parkway had advanced so far when the legislation was passed that the road was never widened beyond sixty feet.) Wide, straight parkways were to connect the three districts, providing not only green space, but light, air, and orderly circulation. Although not all were completely implemented, and some have been poorly maintained, these generous streets continue to grace the life of the inner city.

- *The Great Chicago Fire of 1871*. The fire destroyed most of the core of Chicago, from Twelfth Street to Fullerton Avenue, and prompted many people to move to the areas along the new boulevards being created by the park commissioners. It is no coincidence that many real estate developers also served as commissioners on the three park Boards.

- *The World Columbian Exposition*. The 1893 world's fair enabled the completion of the Midway Plaisance, connecting Jackson and Washington Parks; served as a boost to ordinary citizens' belief in the power of city planning; and fostered a desire for a more sophisticated integration of landscape and architecture in their environment.

- *Daniel Burnham's Plan of Chicago*, published in 1909, which incorporated and extended the historic Boulevard System.[62]

- *The prosperity of the 1920s*. Many previously undeveloped areas along the boulevards were filled in, often with upscale apartment buildings and residences.

- *Consolidation in the 1930s of the three regional park districts into one administrative agency, the Chicago Park District*. Also in this period the Works Progress Administration erected new field houses and multipurpose community buildings in the major squares and parks. Unfortunately, neglect and deterioration beset the parks during World War II and in the postwar period.

- *Reinvestment*. In recent years the Chicago Park District has invested large sums in rehabilitating the Boulevard System and adjoining parks, and local citizens' groups have organized to protect and preserve the landscape and architectural heritage. A Logan Square group, for example, succeeded in persuading the federal government to designate the best preserved two-mile section there as the Logan Square Boulevards Historic District.

From the outset the establishment of the boulevards was a boon to economic development. To persuade wealthy people to buy the high-priced residences along the boulevards (and pay the corresponding taxes) the developers insisted upon beautifully landscaped thoroughfares with convenient connections to parks. Middle-class families purchased town houses with limestone facades, or lived in two- or three-story apartment buildings on adjoining streets. Since the boulevards tended to follow existing commuter lines, convenience of public transportation helped to fuel the boom. Businessmen felt no conflict between their desire for a sound investment and civic idealism—they made money and Chicago gained green space. Today they would call it a "win-win" situation. The results still testify to their sagacity.

At the points where the boulevards turned ninety degrees, various "squares" were created, such as Logan, Palmer, Garfield, and Independence. These spaces were usually landscaped in a formal manner, with allées of trees and geometric layouts, while the adjoining parks were designed in an informal, Olmstedian manner.

Care was taken to install water, gas and sewer pipes in the substructures of the Boulevard System, insuring a high quality of life for the times. In the early days laws intended to ensure that the boulevards were safe, were strictly enforced. Speed limits were set, and commercial vehicles were banned.

From time to time civic-minded donors gave money for commemorative statues: among others, the equestrian figure of George Washington in Washington Square; the *William McKinley Monument* at McKinley Park; and the figure of John A. Logan, a Union general in the Civil War, at Logan Square. In 1995 the city installed stylish kiosks along the boulevards, replete with maps, historic photos, and essays about the surrounding neighborhoods.

Introduction to the West Parks System

Designed by William Le Baron Jenney, and among his greatest achievements, Humboldt, Garfield, and Douglas Parks on the west side were an integral part of the Boulevard System. Planned before the 1871 fire, these parks were seen as a social corrective to the ills of the industrial age. The benefits were many: park were islands of clean air, the "lungs of the city"; they provided places for exercise and recreation; they defused ethnic tensions by bringing together people of different origins; their grassy lawns and quiet pools soothed the nerves; they bolstered real estate development on nearby streets and thus helped increase tax revenues; and they offered local citizens educational and cultural opportunities.[63]

Since the three west parks were considerably smaller (about 180 acres each) than their prototypes in other cities—Central Park in New York, for example, has 844 acres—Jenney tackled the "intermediate" size city park problem with characteristic rigor. Sheep meadows and other large-scale pastoral treatments were not feasible. So Jenney adopted a strategy reminiscent of landscaping around an English country house. Near the house the order is architectonic—formal, symmetrical, with geometric flower beds and trees set in straight lines. As you move into the open countryside, informal, picturesque plantings provide an appropriate transition to the wilds of Mother Nature. Instead of the landscape hiding the buildings, as in a larger park, in these intermediate-size parks buildings are focal points. As such they serve a double function (in addition to housing educational and cultural activities): they are a climax of the vista when seen from a distance, and their terraces provide a platform from which to view yet other vistas.[64]

Jenney planned for the three parks to be harmonious with each other and with the Boulevard System, yet wanted each to have its own distinctive character. Humboldt Park was to be dominated "by an elegant esplanade terminating in a terrace thrust forward into the central lake"; Garfield would be "the most diverse, with athletic fields, a recreational lake, a large conservatory, an arboretum and zoological gardens"; and Douglas would provide "the opportunity to become absorbed in the lush landscape through a series of lakeside promenades with a changing series of water views."[65] Today only some of these differences are discernible, as many modifications have been made over the years.

A fifty-foot column commemorating the centennial of Illinois statehood is the focus of Logan Square (named for Civil War general John A. Logan), the point where the Boulevard System turns south from Logan Boulevard onto Kedzie Boulevard. Surrounded by grassy plots with generous benches, the little park offers views of the neighborhood in several directions.

Like other areas along the boulevards Logan Square developed rapidly during the 1880s and 1890s. It has served as a local commercial center for a succession of working-class immigrants—Scandinavians, Germans, Poles, Russians, and Hispanic Americans. The many homes and apartment buildings on Kedzie Boulevard are given added dignity by the generous setbacks mandated by the 1869 enabling legislation

FIG. 63. People who live nearby have an affection for Logan Square, a frequent site for bridal parties and other celebrations during the warm months.

51   Palmer Square

Palmer and Kedzie Boulevards

Named for Chicago's preeminent real estate and hotel entrepreneur, Potter Palmer, this slender rectangular "square" is enclosed by graystone two-flats and three-flats, some large mansions, and the Old Holy Resurrection Serbian Orthodox Church. Planted with allées of trees, the shady greenway has attracted young urban professionals in recent decades and is host to an annual arts fair.

FIG. 64. A neighborhood focus, Palmer Square is often the site of lively discussions about landmark protection and other neighborhood improvement projects.

52 Humboldt Park

Humboldt and Kedzie Boulevards

See map on pages 190–91. Park north of Refectory or west of Receptory.

Humboldt Park embodies the best of the west parks and Boulevard System. Throngs of people flock to its grounds every day in warm weather, for baseball and soccer games, swimming and fishing, *quinceañeras* and weddings.

The attractions begin with the refectory on the north side of Jens Jensen's broad lagoon, which overlooks the only "beach" in the inner city, a popular spot with the atmosphere of an old swimming hole. Seen from the south, the lagoon and the refectory, with its half-timbered walls, towers, green cupolas, and arches, create a picturesque view. A winding path traces the edge of the lagoon, overhung with willow branches, and bordered by purple blazing liatrice, cattails, arrowroot, and pickerelweed. Water lilies float lazily on its ripples. Small knolls and embankments give the path a gentle rise and fall, withholding some of the views for a time, then revealing surprise enclosures and vistas.

The three spectacular arches of Hugh M. G. Garden's 1907 Boat House (fig. 65) bring together the blue sky and

FIG. 65. In the Humboldt Park Boat House architect Hugh Garden designed arches big enough to embrace a midwestern lagoon under a midwestern sky.

the sparkling water in the finest example of the marriage of landscape and architecture in the Chicago park system. The vista both frames and gives voice to the unique and quintessential qualities of the Midwest landscape: openness and breadth. By placing the strong forms of the Boat House in the open area at the end of the lagoon, Jensen and Garden also gave the whole area a center and a climax. The Boat House has recently been restored, and the lagoon system has been reconnected to the prairie river by Conservation Design Forum.

Continuing south one approaches the Formal Garden and Water Court, and often hears music—this spot is often chosen for *quinceañeras* and weddings (fig. 66). Although red and yellow moss roses have replaced the traditional roses of Jensen's time, their colorful array suits the atmosphere in the now largely Spanish-speaking community. In their monumental survey of the Chicago parks, architects John Vinci and Phillip Hamp and landscape architect Stephen F. Christy write, concerning the formal garden:

FIG. 66. Elegant and symmetrical, the open pavilion of the Formal Garden in Humboldt Park is the setting for many spring and summer weddings. An artful fusion of Chicago architecture and landscape, the site also features a water court and elaborate floral displays.

Its simplicity of design and execution make it one of the great works of American landscape architecture. Jensen purposefully lowered its elevation several feet and erected earthen berms and heavy plantings around it for two reasons. The first was to give it a special air of separation and wholeness, made possible by the screening and the ability of the visitor to look down on the entire area at a glance. The second was a corollary of the first: to make it totally unobtrusive to the large landscape beyond. Jensen was trying to weave the rest of the park into a landscape suggestive of native Illinois, and he wanted the formality and striking

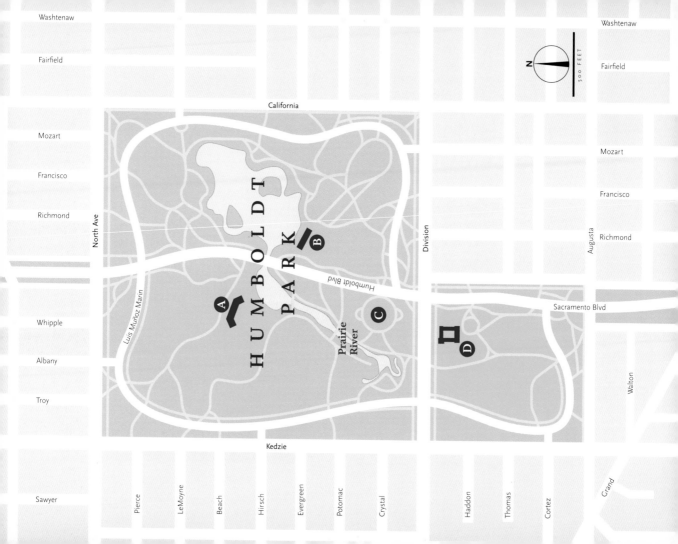

Humboldt Park

A. Refectory
B. Boat House
C. Formal Garden/Water Court
D. Receptory and Stable

appearance of the Rose Garden to pass unseen except for those who sought it out.[66]

The plan of this garden was published and became well known shortly after its completion. Essentially it is a large circle bisected by a water court and flanked by pavilions in cast concrete. Square columns support an openwork trellis overhead. The central pavilion, opposite the entrance, is curved, the flanking pavilions are straight. When the flowers are at their height and the waters of the fountain dapple the surface of the pond, the area has a magical quality.

On the south side of the park, acting like an anchor, is the so-called Receptory and Stable, by Frommann and Jebsen (1896). Of red brick with maroon steeples and steeply pitched gables, it has the air of an old Norwegian hunting lodge, recalling an earlier group of immigrants that settled this part of Chicago (just across the street is the Norwegian American Hospital). This part of the lagoon system is rich in botanical diversity—white oak, basswood, redbud, yellow flag iris, bulrush, and water lilies.

Humboldt Park is also home to a large collection of sculpture, including two bison by Edward Kemeys (best known for the lions at the entrance to the Art Institute of Chicago); figures of Leif Erickson by Sigvald Asbjornsen, Alexander von Humboldt by Felix Gorling, and Fritz Reuter by Franz Englemann; and *The Miner and Child,* by Charles J. Mulligan.

A detour from the Boulevard System, the Chicago Center for Green Technology is of interest to all green technology advocates. The building has retained the boxy contours of the old factory out of which it was fashioned, because adaptive reuse is part of its raison d'etre. The CCGT is one of the first buildings in the United states to receive a Leadership in Energy and Environmental Design (LEED) Platinum rating, the highest awarded by the United States Green Building Council.

The building, redesigned by architect Douglas Farr in 2002, with backing from both the city of Chicago and the American Institute of Architects, has several energy conserving features: an elevator that runs on canola oil rather than soil-polluting hydraulic oil; energy-generating solar panels; insulated windows; cisterns that collect rainwater for use in watering the plants in the garden; and a retention pond to reduce storm runoff. The floors are made from recycled rubber tires; newspaper combines with gypsum for the drywall; the linoleum is made of linseed oil; and the carpeting is in movable squares so that those that get the most wear can periodically be switched with those in less traveled areas.

The slanted parking lot channels water into a prairie garden; the garden on the roof, designed to counter the effect of an urban heat island, not only offers a view of the Chicago skyline but provides insulation, keeping the building cooler in summer and warmer in winter. What appears to be soil is a mixture of clay, shale, ash, and paper, a lightweight mixture that has been planted with sedums and succulents. These plants hold water in their leaves, not their roots, so only five inches of soil are needed to sustain them. Birds and butterflies visit the gardens regularly.

In tours of the building, guides are likely to explain that the green design movement, which has taken off in Europe, was an inspiration to Mayor Richard M. Daley. Returning from a trip to Frankfurt, Germany, the mayor ordered his Department of the Environment to give Chicago more green roofs. New municipal buildings must now conform to some degree to LEED standards. All new libraries participate in the program, as do some police stations, public housing structures, and parking lots. Some cultural institutions and private corporations are following suit. The Art Institute's new wing by Renzo Piano will have a green roof. The Medical and Dental Arts Building already has one, and since Millennium Park is over a parking garage, some say it is the largest green roof in the United States.

Bounded by Kinzie Street, Congress Boulevard, and Hamlin and Homan Avenues

See map on pages 196–97.

The visitor entering Garfield Park at Washington Boulevard and Homan Avenue is greeted by the sweeping panorama of William Le Baron Jenney's lagoons, a vista that culminates in the golden dome of the Administration Building in the west. Here we see two strands of Chicago's history woven together in a surprisingly pleasing ensemble: a 1928 Beaux Arts "Spanish Baroque" building, by Michaelsen and Rognstad, set in an 1871 prairie landscape. Purists might wish away the monumentality of the building, and the glitter of its dome, as at odds with the horizontality and earth tones of the prairie, but to me it seems quintessentially Chicago. The city as a whole is also a soaring structure set at the edge of expansive grasslands (now mostly wheat, corn, and soybeans), punctuated with meandering rivers.

The horizontal branches of the hawthorns along the entrance drive are more obviously at home in the prairie and lead to the waterscape beyond, edged in turn with low-lying plants. Crowning the views in every direction are fabulous burr oak trees, many of them over a hundred years old, in all probability specified by Jenney, as early photographs of the site show a treeless plain. The thick bark of burr oaks resists lightning and fire; the deep roots allow these trees to endure weeks of deep frost, freezing winds, and months of drought—good, tough midwestern characteristics.

Continuing on, J. L. Silsbee's exotic bandstand brings a playful Saracen touch to the landscape. Its lively roof silhouette, octagonal profile, and sparkling white marble are adorned with colored-glass mosaics. The whole is also elevated five feet above the hundred-foot-wide marble concourse that surrounds it. Beyond are symmetrical lawns, recalling ancient Indian gardens. Apparently when first erected the bandstand and the surrounding grounds were illuminated entirely by electric lights, which must have enchanted evening visitors to concerts and other events.

North of the bandstand, and just south of Madison Street, is a formal garden with a pavilion and benches designed by a Prairie School architect, probably Hugh M. G. Garden. The unadorned but well-proportioned pergola is

GARFIELD PARK

A. Conservatory
B. Administration Building
C. Bandstand
D. Formal Garden and Pavilion

inviting and spacious in a rectilinear mode. The benches might have been inspired by the Oak Park studio of Frank Lloyd Wright. This complex is in marked contrast to Silsbee's confection, a reminder that Wright and his contemporaries were active in the same period as the Beaux Arts architects coming out of the World's Columbian Exposition.

When we think of landscape architecture of the Prairie School we think of Jens Jensen and his informal lagoons, indigenous plants, and limestone council circles, but there is another aspect of this period that more resembles the Secessionist gardens of turn-of-the-century Vienna. This garden style favors small articulated areas, architectonic in approach, with a preference for straight instead of curved lines, and a desire to define outdoor rooms by means of arbors, pergolas, and other architectural elements.[67]

In the broad open meadow to the southwest Jensen captures another aspect of the spirit of the heartland—the place where forests and prairies meet. The trees approach the grasslands at the edges but interrupt their peaceful expanses with only an occasional grove of tall verticals, recalling the primeval savannas of the ancient Midwest. Jensen's deepest exploration of the region's geological heritage, however, appears north of the lagoons in the park's magnificent conservatory.

Garfield Park Conservatory
Central Park Avenue and Fulton Boulevard

Pitched to recall a haystack, the roof of the Garfield Park Conservatory, designed by Jens Jensen and executed by engineers Hitching & Co. in 1907-8, is tall, handsome, and as unadorned as an Illinois farmer. Inside, however, Jensen's stunning and sophisticated "landscapes under glass" unfold before the visitor. The first, the great Palm House, sets the tropical tone. Several ceiling-high great palms shelter us and punctuate the lush vegetation on all sides. Here and there, great thinkers are brought momentarily into our company through quotations mounted on waist high standards. Buddha, for example:

> The forest is a peculiar organism of unlimited kindness and benevolence that makes no demands for its sustenance and extends generously the products of its life and activity. It affords protection to all being.

Straight ahead is the Fern Room, a succession of geological allusions (fig. 67). Descending six feet, Jensen's

FIG. 67. A world-class masterpiece, the Fern Room at the Garfield Park Conservatory is a deep-time mirror reflecting Chicago's botanical past—all the way back to the age of the dinosaurs.

metaphor for going back in time, we enter a tropical landscape evoking the era before the continents now in the western hemisphere split from those of the eastern hemisphere, a time before the ice age when Illinois lay next to the equator. An elliptical path leads around a large central lagoon, with islands of ancient cycads and ferns—species that predate the dinosaurs—arranged to luscious effect. On the outer edges of the room, Jensen piled up layer after layer of stratified limestone, to simulate the cliffs that towered throughout Illinois before the leveling action of the great glaciers. The rock work is extensive and intricate, creating overhanging ledges, dark pools, and small waterfalls. Softening the surfaces of the rocks, and adding to the impression of the primeval, are moist green mosses and lichens. One hears water trickling from hidden sources. Here and there it bubbles forth, gathering in rivulets, puddling into small ponds. All of this suggests the ancient rock formations, the mineral sources of the prairies, and the birth of the first rivers that coursed their way through the grasslands. It is a poem in praise of the gifts of the past to the present, and in my opinion one of the greatest of American works of art.

As Michael LaCoste, an intern who worked on the field verification of this book in 2005 wrote in his log:

> The pitched roof of the Fern Room is also reflected in the pool, forming a diamond shape, leading the viewer to perceive the space as the conservatory's jewel. . . . There is an interweaving of the structure and the plants, the shell and its contents, the manmade and the natural, where each affects and enhances the other.

Our thoughts turn to the future as we read a Kashmiri proverb on a plaque further on:

> We have not inherited the world from our forefathers, we have borrowed it from our children.

The conservatory's other chambers re-create a variety of different worlds—a Children's Garden, a Desert House, an Aroid House, a Show House. Red bananas, vanilla orchids, chocolate trees bearing the "fruit of the gods," a small sugarcane grove, and pineapple plants turn the Sweet House into an ambrosial feast—one big dessert.

55 Columbus Park

*Bounded by Central Avenue, Austin Boulevard, Adams Street,
and the Eisenhower Expressway (Interstate 290)*

*See map on pages 202–3. Park on west side of Golf Drive.
A worthwhile west-side detour from the Boulevard System.*

As you pass between the entrance lanterns on Jackson
Boulevard at Central Street, you begin a journey through
another of Jens Jensen's great representations of midwestern prairies. Jensen cherished the notion that Chicago
had grown on the banks of a prairie river, at the edge of
an alluring vastness:

> For years the message of our great prairies had appealed
> to me. Every leisure moment found me trampling through
> unspoiled bits of these vast areas. I wanted to understand
> their force, their enchantment that called on and on. Then
> came the opportunity to build a large park on the prairies,
> at the edge of a great metropolis. No one can realize what
> such an opportunity meant to me at that time in my life.[68]

FIG. 68. Jens Jensen's stone work in Columbus Park reflects the origins
of prairie rivers in the merging of many small streams flowing through
the limestone beds of the Midwest.

N

500 FEET

Pine

Monroe

Adams

Quincy

Jackson

Gladys

Van Buren

Congress

Harrison

Flournoy

Central

Parkside

Waller

Menard

Mayfield

Mason

Austin

Madison

Field House

C

Prairie River

A

B

Golf Dr

Golf Course

C O L U M B U S   P A R K

I-290

Eisenhower Expwy

Railroad

Arthington

Menard

Monitor

Mayfield

Mason

Fillmore

Humphrey

Adams

Jackson

Van Buren

Harrison

Lyman

CTA Blue Line
Austin station

Humphrey

Lyman

COLUMBUS PARK

A. Refectory
B. River Springs
C. Council Ring

To distill the essence of the prairie in a work of art—this was Jensen's challenge to himself. The essentials were clear: a gentle terrain bordered by bluffs, a vast meadow of flowering grasses cut by slowly meandering rivers and edged with lush native plantings, the whole interrupted by occasional groves of trees.

In designing Columbus Park, Jensen made a largely unbroken expanse the center of his plan. To hide the encroaching city he placed hawthorn trees around the perimeter. Inserted into this fabric were other park features: an "old swimming hole," a player's green, and a council ring.

Today it takes some historic imagination to re-create Jensen's 1918 vision. A golf course has been placed on the prairie meadow, for example, so the expanse is mowed fairways and manicured green instead of a waving grassland, but some of the vastness is still there. The Refectory, by Chatten & Hammond, is not in the Prairie School style Jensen would probably have specified, but it is nevertheless a handsome building and has become a popular community center. Its main room is lined by arches overlooking the lagoon, and the airy arcade of the south loggia unites the prairie river, the golf course, and a terrace with a certain grandeur that is not totally alien to Jensen's conception.

The limestone ledges that mark the source of Jensen's springs (which later merge to form the prairie river) have been sensitively restored by the Chicago Park District (fig. 68). A recent grant awarded to the Chicago Park District by Save America's Treasures (through the efforts of Julia Sniderman Bachrach) will be used to restore a Prairie School shelter, stone paths, the council ring, and appropriate plants materials.

56 Douglas Park

Bounded by Roosevelt Road, Nineteenth Street, and Albany and California Avenues
(enter at Douglas Boulevard and Albany Avenue)

See map on pages 206–7. Park on street parallel to and just south of Ogden Avenue.

If you want to get a feeling for Chicago's inner city, you should visit the third of Jenney's west parks, Douglas Park, on a summer day. In June architect Hugh M. G. Garden's Flower Hall, in the southern half of the park, is often the site of, for example, a dance performance by Najwa Dance Corps, from Malcolm X College, or an African American wedding. It is an exquisite setting for a wedding. The central pavilion (fig. 69) is crowned with a majestic arch, bordered by a trellis, and flanked by five open bays on either side, with smaller pavilions at each end. Refreshments can be served on both sides, and the formal garden to the east, with its sparkling fountain in a reflecting pool, bordered by colorful flowers, pleasantly accommodates mingling guests. At the far end are Prairie School style benches set in a semicircle, appropriate spots for grandparents and other dignitaries. Not to be missed is the lawn and small pond with twelve spectacular weeping willows just to the northeast. From the far side of the willows note the long axial view back to the pavilion.

FIG. 69. A stately semicircular arch crowns the pergola at the southern entrance of Douglas Park—another frequent scene of bridal parties.

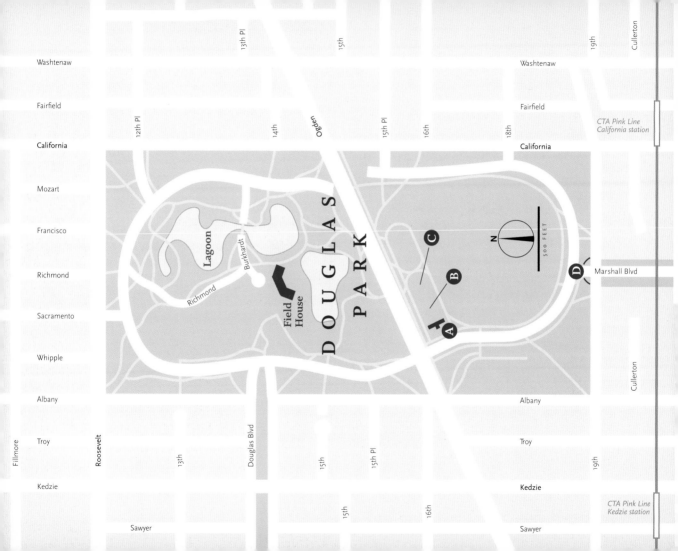

Douglas Park

A. Flower Hall
B. Central Pavilion
C. Formal Garden
D. Pergola

A large berm separates this area from the great meadow to the south. Jensen specified hawthorns to define and surround the meadow, now a field where children play baseball and soccer, and some are still in place.

In the northeastern part of the park some of Jenney's original lagoon system is still intact, but the intrusion of a large school has changed the section's character. At the southern entrance, on Nineteenth Street, Douglas Park is given monumentality by a stately semicircular pergola. Framing a vista of the large meadow beyond, the ensemble is another example of combination of landscape and architectural forms in the west side park system.

3555 West Ogden Avenue

Lawndale was once one of the liveliest, most densely settled areas in Chicago, but it suffered the loss of its commercial base in the 1960s, and in subsequent years much of its building stock deteriorated, drug dealing spread, and crime increased. In the 1980s a group of local citizens, designating themselves Slumbusters, began converting the vacant lots that littered the community into gardens. One couple, Lorean and Gerald Earles, took a leadership role in their block at 1900 South Trumbull Avenue. "We would clean up over the weekends, and the city would pick up the trash on Mondays," Gerald Earles told me. "We wanted the vacant lot next to our place to look good, but it was more than that. We wanted the whole neighborhood to look good; it is part of the education of our children." Gradually the slumbuster movement grew, and today the neighborhood is filled with gardens and signs posted by the many block clubs that sponsor them. On Saturdays you can see volunteers doing the necessary planting, weeding, and hoeing in vegetable patches and flower gardens. Perhaps, as cultural geographers have

FIG. 70. High school students Paris Wright and Dexter Sullivan display a "before" picture of the lot they helped transform into a garden in North Lawndale, one of several Green Youth Farms jointly sponsored by the Neighborhood Housing Services of Chicago and the Chicago Botanic Garden.

suggested, having "nature nearby is a material and symbolic gateway to a better world."[69]

To support this community effort the Chicago Botanic Garden has set up the Green Youth Farm program in cooperation with Neighborhood Housing Services of Chicago. Basically a summer work-training program, it teaches local teens about urban agriculture, healthy eating, business skills, and teamwork while helping to improve the community. Principles of good gardening, such as succession planting, organic crops, and square-foot planting have yielded bumper crops of peppers, cabbages, beans, watermelons, tomatoes, cucumbers, lettuces, squash, pumpkin, eggplant, and corn under the care of teens (fig. 70). Other examples include the African American Garden at Twelfth Place and Central Park Avenue; a Seniors Garden at 3800 West Arthington Street, near the Homan Square Community Center, locus of the Lawndale community transformation; and the Polk Street Block Club at 3800 West Polk Street. In 2002 the Field Museum hosted an exhibition featuring twelve local community gardens.[70]

Bounded by Thirty-seventh Street, Pershing Road, and Western and Damen Avenues

As the pace of industrialization increased in Chicago, the pressures of urban life grew. Between 1870 and 1890 the city's population more than tripled, from 298,977 to 1,099,850. Working-class families living near the stockyards, brickyards, or iron and steel plants where they worked were unable to get to the large landscaped parks on a regular basis, and, given the crowded conditions of their neighborhoods, had few places to enjoy fresh air, to play and exercise, or to find educational and cultural opportunities. Health and sanitation problems, labor unrest, concern about child labor, and the potential for ethnic conflict soared, driving leading citizens of the period to call for a different kind of park in Chicago. Parks became an important part of the social reform efforts of the period.

McKinley Park was the first park constructed in the era of Chicago's small neighborhood park movement. Although it is not distinguished in its design, it had play-

grounds, ball fields, a swimming lagoon, and a modest field house (fig. 71). Its success helped to foster the creation of more than a dozen other neighborhood parks in the following decades. Today McKinley Park's rehabilitated lagoon is a popular fishing area. The park also boasts an interactive water playground and an ice-skating rink.

FIG. 71. McKinley Park's lagoon is a popular fishing area in the summer and a magnet for ice skaters in the winter.

Bounded by Garfield Boulevard, Fifty-second and Loomis Streets, and Racine Avenue

Sherman Park successfully combines features of the naturalistic character of the great landscaped parks of the late nineteenth century and the small neighborhood parks of the early-twentieth-century Reform Era. A jewel in the Chicago park system, its three major design elements—a circular lagoon, an island meadow, and a handsome field house—are unified and mutually enhancing (fig. 72). This ensemble was the result of the cooperation of two firms. D. H. Burnham and Company designed the field house, and the Olmsted Brothers were the landscape architects.

The parts are held together and enclosed by a high berm that separates the park from the busy city streets. The melding of the classical symmetry of the building with the pastoral informality of the landscaping is brought about by placing a rectangular terrace with an entry court and pergola between the building and the lagoon. The ensemble indicates that both passive leisure activities and structured programs can be gracefully accommodated. As Vinci, Christy, and Hamp note, it is "one of those rare works of landscape art that looks perfect from every angle."

Recent efforts by the Chicago Park District have restored the field house's original green Spanish tile roof, reconstructed the pergolas, matched the original windows, and upgraded the plant materials.

FIG. 72. Sherman Park (Chicago Park District Special Collections)

Bounded by Seventy-second and Seventy-fourth Streets, Parnell Avenue, and the Metra tracks

Hamilton Park is another good example of the small neighborhood park movement in Chicago just after the turn of the twentieth century, and the combined work of D. H. Burnham and Company and the Olmsted Brothers. An aerial view (fig. 73) shows how the park is integrated into its surroundings—single-family houses, apartment flats, and the local school. At first the people living nearby were not sure they wanted all of the recreational facilities the other parks had, asserting that they wanted an ornamental park, but they soon changed their minds.[71] Today the park has the full complement: gymnasiums, playground, tennis courts, and other amenities.

FIG. 73. An aerial photograph (circa 1930) shows the need for open space in the crowded south-side neighborhood around Hamilton Park.

61 Washington Park
Bounded by Hyde Park and Cottage Grove Avenues, Sixtieth Street, and Martin Luther King Drive
See map on pages 216–17.

Washington Park was once the best example of Olmsted and Vaux's work in Chicago (fig. 74), but much of the original plan has been altered and given over to the automobile. The speeding traffic alters the ambiance to the extent that the park should be viewed as a collection of fragments of the original design.

As you enter on Garfield Boulevard you see that Olmsted and Vaux took advantage of an old glacial ridge to enclose the west side of the park, and used the excavated dirt from the lagoon to form a complementary berm on the east. Between is a gently rolling "sheep meadow," the largest unbroken expanse in the Chicago park system, shaded on its borders by magnificent groves of trees. Olmsted described his vision: "The visitor, as he passes through the outer grove, will find a view opening before him over a greensward without a perceptible break . . . and ending in one direction in a glimmer of water reflecting tall trees nearly a mile away."[72] The water is in the extensive lagoon system in the southern half of the park. In the original

plan, the lagoons were to draw water from Lake Michigan via a canal (what is now the Midway Plaisance), but that would have required their being dug deeper.

This section of the park is carefully contoured so that as you follow its paths small hillocks block out the surrounding city. The goal is clearly to give you a day in the country, or in a picturesque countryside, with charming

bridges connecting the lagoons, a leafy canopy protecting you from the sun, wildflowers blooming in the meadows, and grassy islands within the lagoons.

Dusable Museum of African American History
740 East Fifty-sixth Place

Now a museum devoted to African-American history, honoring the population surrounding Washington Park, this D. H. Burnham and Company building is ornamented with classical swags, pilasters, and architraves. Like other Burnham buildings in Olmsted landscapes, it has a formal garden on the north side to ease the transition from symmetry to informality. The sunken garden is filled in summer with circles of sunflowers, black-eyed Susans, marigolds, and other perennials.

FIG. 74. Washington Park in its early years was the epitome of the informal English approach to park design. Frederick Law Olmstead inserted a sheep meadow to the north not only to provide a pastoral touch but to keep the grass "mowed."

Burnham's refectory of 1911, now called the Pool Building, is on the west side, and centers on a geometrical complex of swimming pools, a spray pool, and a wading pool. The Tuscan columns enclosing the generous loggia, and the four stately towers at the corners of the central section once housed park district offices but now comprise locker rooms for swimmers and rooms for parties and other special events.

Washington Park joins the Midway Plaisance at Cottage Grove Avenue. The transition is marked by Lorado Taft's 1922 sculpture *The Fountain of Time* and a reflecting pool (under restoration at this writing). This massive work, depicting a hundred people in varying postures of work and weariness, was supposedly inspired by lines from a poem by Austin Dobson:

> Time goes, you say? Ah no!
> Alas, time stays; we go.

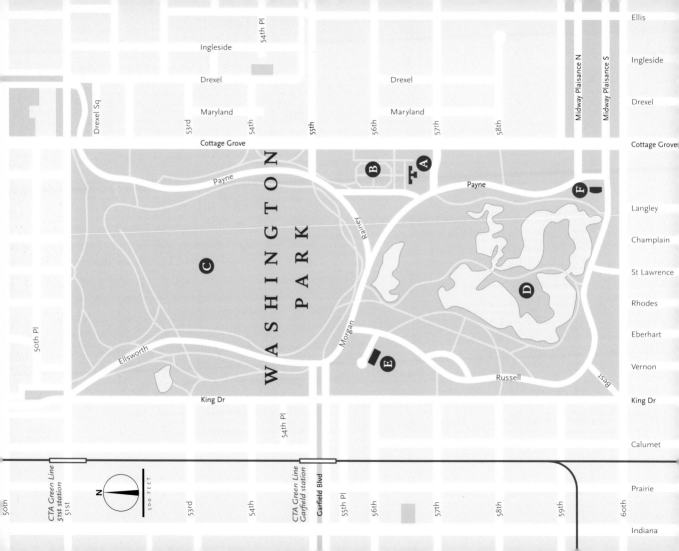

Washington Park

A. DuSable Museum
B. Formal Garden
C. Sheep Meadow
D. Lagoon
E. Pool Building
F. *Fountain of Time*

62 Drexel Boulevard

Canal Street, from Lake Street to Jackson Boulevard

This broad boulevard, just northeast of Washington Park, once stood as the acme of the Boulevard System (fig. 75). In its prime, dignified gray limestone houses formed a handsome border along both sides of the wide parklike space, and the median provided meandering walkways, shaded by tall trees and ornamented with flowering shrubs and plants, with an occasional fountain or piece of sculpture to give further definition to this graceful urban space.

FIG. 75. A boulevard is a hybrid of a street and a park. The completion of Drexel Boulevard was an economic boon to the neighborhood, as people wanted to build houses near a broad green with trees and flowers.

The Midway Plaisance, between Washington and Jackson Parks, was intended as a link to the surrounding neighborhoods and, as part of the Boulevard System, to the rest of the city, but with increased traffic it gradually turned into a hazardous roadway.

Since it cuts through the University of Chicago campus, the university has cooperated with the Chicago Park District, the city, and south-side community leaders on a new Midway Plaisance Master Plan, which aims to change the Midway from expressway to stroll way.[73] The goal is to lower the speed of traffic, increase safety, and develop several gardens, such as a "reader's garden," a winter garden, a health and healing garden (near the hospital complex), a children's garden, a skating rink and warming house, and an urban horticulture center. Some of the plans have already been realized, helping connect Hyde Park and Woodlawn residents with each other. Some residents have complained about the loss of the former grandeur of the uninterrupted sweep of the Midway, while others maintain the new recreational and social connections are worth the sacrifice.

To attract pedestrians from Jackson Park to the Midway, the viaduct under the Metra railway will be repaired and the forest of Moorish arches that support the tracks adorned with red stripes, fiber optics, and pin spotlights. When the transformation is complete, the illuminated surfaces may turn this connecting link into a destination in its own right. This idea exemplifies a more general forward-looking spirit that strives to transform bridges and other transitional spaces into landscapes.

The plant materials, recreational opportunities, and street furniture of the future Midway will provide a background blanket of green that will unite town and gown, inviting the neighbors to partake of seasonable pleasures on or near the university grounds.

Lake Meadows and Prairie Shores

East of Martin Luther King Jr. Drive, between Thirty-first and Thirty-fifth Streets (Lake Meadows)
and Twenty-seventh and Thirtieth Streets (Prairie Shores)

An entry park graces the northeast corner of Lake Meadows, one of America's most successful mixed-race, privately owned rental-housing complexes. Gently contoured topography, shaded by honey locusts, ash, and Japanese maples, all in beds outlined by French curves, state at the outset that this is a landscaped world. The luxurious, carefully maintained lawns between the buildings suggest a suburban country club (fig. 76). The effect is intentional; part of the plan was to lure people in from outlying areas, or to persuade them to stay, to help counter the postwar trend toward "white flight" of the period.[74]

The idea that the problems of overcrowding and other urban ills could be solved by high-rise residential towers placed in broad open parks was first advanced by the French architect Le Corbusier in the 1920s and 1930s. Soon translated into English, his books *Towards a New Architecture, The City of Tomorrow and Its Planning,* and *The Radiant City* were internationally influential. Corbusier's ideal urban design included not only residential towers but accompanying stores, schools, and other ancillary buildings. Generous parks were part of every illustration.

FIG. 76. Placing clusters of high-rise apartments within a park was an idea first advanced by French architect Le Corbusier. In most large cities the concept has failed. Its success at Lake Meadows, a racially mixed housing complex in Chicago, is thought-provoking.

Fairly or unfairly, Corbusier's concept was later blamed for the crowding of public housing and its general failure. Many units were subsequently demolished, including the infamous Pruitt-Igoe public housing complex in Saint Louis and more recently, three Chicago Housing Authority high-rises only a mile south of Lake Meadows. Most critics blamed the architects or the design idea, yet few pointed out that the original plans, including Minoru Yamasaki's for Pruitt-Igoe, included playgrounds and gardens that were deemed too expensive and never built by the developers. After the Saint Louis buildings were imploded and the debris carried away in 1972, residential towers fell out of favor as a public housing model, but that is part of another story. At the end of World War II Corbusier's vision was already implanted in the minds of the architectural generation then active. In Chicago, Mies van der Rohe's recently completed Promontory Apartments provided a successful model.[75]

Lake Meadows was one of the first residential projects planned by the New York Life Insurance Company to take advantage of new government subsidies and liberal tax concessions to help clear the urban blight facing the nation at the end of the war. The Chicago architecture firm Skidmore, Owings & Merrill was selected for the seventy-acre lot between Thirty-first and Thirty-fifth Streets along what was then Grand Boulevard (now Martin Luther King Jr. Drive). The designated principal designer was Ambrose Richardson; the SOM landscape architect was Beatrice Horneman.[76]

Ten high-rise apartment buildings, a shopping center, recreational facilities, a clubhouse, and an office building rose by the end of the 1950s. It is important to note that only 8 percent of the site was used for buildings, leaving 92 percent for parkland and parking lots. The land surrounding the buildings was contoured for a practical reason—to hide the parking lots. Trees were then planted to screen the wire fencing of the tennis courts. Architect Walter Netsch said, "It was not a sophisticated landscape design, but it turned out to have a nice aura. One of the reasons was the large scale. The idea was that it was a meadow by the lake. We were interested in openness. Owings did not want the closely packed quality of the near north side."[77]

Racially integrated from the start, Lake Meadows has been an outstanding success. Fully occupied and in good condition more than fifty years later, the complex exemplifies the idea that a mixed racial population can live comfortably in skyscrapers set in green parkland—living proof of the validity of Corbusier's dream on Chicago's south side. What does this mean in the face of widespread international opinion that such arrangements are doomed to failure?

Another urban renewal project, initiated by Michael Reese Hospital, is Prairie Shores, the complex of apartment buildings just north of Lake Meadows. Designed by architects Loebl, Schlossman and Bennett and landscape architects Stephanie S. Kramer and Sasaki and Peter Walker (1959–62), it comprises five nineteen-story buildings laid out in a zigzag plan, to provide lake views to the maximum number of residents. From a distance, the buildings provide a glass screen that unites the whole complex. Up close, these handsome vertical accents define the space and enclose the shared parklands below.

The successes of these two housing complexes have been carefully studied by social scientists. In a series of scholarly papers, the Institute of Behavior and Environment, a group centered at the University of Illinois at Urbana-Champaign, demonstrated that proximity to well-maintained parkland helps develop self-discipline in girls, reduces aggression and violence in all children, helps lower crime rates, increases informal contact among neighbors, and is a productive focus for community organization.[78]

ACCESS CAN BE VISUAL OR PHYSICAL. In my own fieldwork I was puzzled that I saw few people in the spacious parks at Lake Meadows, even on summer weekends, but I only visited four times. As an art historian, I know that landscape is a visual representation as well as a social opportunity, and that access can be visual as well as physical. In informal interviews some residents told me that just looking at the green space was important to them. One woman I found waiting for a bus (wearing a T-shirt emblazoned "Lake Meadows") said she was a social worker who had lived in the complex for years. In her words:

At the time I moved in the population was about 70 percent black, 30 percent other. The park has never been used much. Just for kids playing, or a community picnic once a year, which is never much of a success. Looking at it, on the other hand, from my fourth floor balcony, I always have the feeling that all my work has amounted to something. I like to have friends over in the daytime on weekends so they can look out my windows and see the treetops and the lawns and flowers below. I guess you could say the park, being so well kept up, is a kind of status symbol. People are proud to live here. And there's no graffiti or litter, ever.[79]

It seems that simply having a view of urban nature is a symbol of status and a source of contentment.

Many questions beyond the scope of this book remain to be answered about Lake Meadows and Prairie Shores. Just how significant has the decision to give much of the property over to well-landscaped parkland been in the success of these high-rise complexes? Is anything inherently wrong with Corbusier's idea? Perhaps the failures of other urban high-rise developments were due not to the architectural but to the social planning. Many experts believe that poor maintenance of the landscaping was one of the reasons for the failure of some public housing projects in Chicago, especially the now nearly completely demolished Stateway Gardens. Answers to these questions await more research.

PART VIII

CHICAGO BOTANIC GARDEN

1000 Lake Cook Road, Glencoe, Illinois

A map is available at the visitor center.

The Chicago Botanic Garden is the eighth wonder of Chicago.

The work of this remarkable institution, owned by the Forest Preserve District of Cook County and managed by the Chicago Horticultural Society, extends deeply into the fabric of Chicago, which is visible on the horizon from its visitor center (fig. 77). As already noted, its Neighborhood Gardens Project has affected Pullman, North Lawndale, and many other neighborhoods in the inner city.

A series of distinguished architects and landscape architects—beginning with John Ormsbee Simonds and Geoffrey Rausch, who drafted the master plan in 1964—have added to the attractions of this natural lagoon system over the last four decades. The combined efforts of highly civilized trustees and professional management have made it the unrivaled diva of midwestern landscape.

Three areas celebrate the three primal ecologies of Illinois—the Dixon Prairie, the Mary Mix McDonald Woods, and the Skokie River Wetland; all are managed but not "designed." The twenty-five designed additions include the esplanade, one of Dan Kiley's last works (with his associate Peter Morrow Meyer), and the gardens highlighting particular types of flora, landscapes and conditions, and aesthetic traditions. There are also a model railroad garden, a children's museum, and many seasonal displays, such as the bonsai exhibition.

With map in hand, visitors may plan their day according to the season and the weather. The heritage garden, a tribute to botany and the display of plants, is on the way to the education center. This building, designed by architect Edward Larabee Barnes (1975), houses the greenhouses and special exhibitions. It has a spectacular fountain and views of the north lawn, and forms, with Kiley's esplanade—a fine example of the fusion of landscape architecture and architecture.

A favorite route turns next to the English walled garden by landscape architect John Brookes. Following along the path

FIG. 77. The Chicago skyline is just visible on the horizon in this aerial view of the Chicago Botanic Garden, but the highway linking city and park is evident. Typical of midwestern ecology, the site has the profusion of both Eastern Woodland trees and prairie flora, with an abundance of slow-flowing water in its lagoon system.

GREAT BASIN, CHICAGO BOTANIC GARDEN

to the English oak meadow one has a view of one of the triumphs of the garden, the Great Basin by Oehm, Van Sweden & Associates (2002). This homage to the prairie captures the essence of the wet prairie, near the water's edges, and the dry prairie, higher up its sloping banks. A spirit of boundlessness, appropriate to the prairies, permeates the atmosphere: the great pond acts as foreground and captures the reflection of the clouds and the bright blue of the midwestern sky.

The pond, in reality a seven-and-a-half-acre flood storage lagoon, has as its focus Evening Island, with its five acres of gently undulating terrain. An open lawn in the center is given definition by broad beds of perennials at the edges, and they, in turn, give way to a shady alder grove with various thickly planted ground covers. Caesar's Brother, a blue iris, threads through the different areas the way clover does in the prairies today. The west knoll is grassland, the east knoll descends from dappled shade to a sunny hillside. There is Jens Jensen–inspired council ring too.[80]

Returning east, the three islands of Sansho-en, the Japanese garden, offer an authentic oriental experience seldom encountered outside Japan. Landscape architect Koichi Kawana finished the initial design in 1982, beginning with the beautiful entrance bridge to Keunto, the first island. A tranquil teahouse is settled in a small moss garden of its own, frequently misted, of course, and on some Sundays tea ceremonies are performed here. A divided path leads across the water to Seifuto island, which hosts the House of Pure Clean Breezes at its summit. Finally, across the way, is Horaijima, the island of Everlasting Happiness, which one may see but not visit, at least not in this life.

A highlight of the walk back toward the education center is the forty-five-foot waterfall cascade. Beyond that are the rose garden; Spider Island, by Michael Van Valkenburgh; the aquatic garden, with sumptuous water lilies and lotus blossoms; and the bulb, native plant, and fruit and vegetable gardens.

North of the education center, walk down through the trees to the semicircular stone terrace where the garden meets the water.[81] Here the visitor should turn around for a view back toward a double allée of elm trees sloping upward to the building's expansive, handsome arms—a fitting climax to the visit.

Conclusion
Envisioning the Future

Any conclusion regarding the dynamic processes described in this book must inevitably be arbitrary. The merger of architecture and landscape that began in Chicago in the nineteenth century will continue indefinitely in the future. As we go to press, plans are on the drawing boards for developing more of the old industrial area around Lake Calumet into a vast new public space. Some industrial uses will continue, but in a new, greener environment. Hegewisch Marsh, on the far southeast side, is being cleaned up by local volunteers to allow access to the prairie, wetland, and wooded environments there. A twenty-four-thousand-square-foot visitors facility is being planned.[82] Stearns Quarry, also on the south side, in Bridgeport, is scheduled for transformation into a large preserve. Rich in fossils, the quarry's limestone walls expose remnants of Silurian bedrock and ancient coral reefs. New trails will provide educational opportunities for exploring the 350-foot-deep site, and an athletic field, fishing pier, and other structures will enrich the neighborhood's outdoor opportunities

Public-private cooperation is already in place for creating a linear park along three miles of abandoned Bloomingdale Line train tracks on the northwest side of the city. Even the area under the el tracks in the Loop is being redesigned with vibrant lighting and landscaping.

In 2006, the University of Illinois at Chicago dedicated Gateway Plaza, designed by sculptor James Turrell, at Halsted Street and Roosevelt Road. The centerpiece of the landscaped site is Turrell's *Skyspace,* an elliptical chamber with an oculus open to the sky. Likely to become one of the most satisfying works of public art in the city, *Skyspace* will be accessible to people day and night.[83]

To facilitate the merger of the natural world with the built environment, educational institutions are becoming more interdisciplinary, requiring architects and landscape architects to learn from each other and to cooperate as early in the planning processes as possible. Public officials now solicit input from private providers and local communities at the outset of each new project. Enlightened businessmen increasingly recognize the benefits of supporting public spaces. If these trends continue, unhampered by catastrophic economic or social ills, the results can serve as a model for other cities and for the future.

One reason for the success in Chicago is the political climate. In other cities local governments have relinquished their watchdog role in protecting the public domain. When this happens, developers pressure architects to cut costs, and the losses are frequently the public green spaces. Under pressure from developer Bruce Ratner, Renzo Piano eliminated the elegant rooftop garden he had specified for the top of the New York Times tower. The same developer forced Frank Gehry to turn what was to have been a public garden on the roof of a new arena in the Atlantic Yards project in Brooklyn into a private garden and running track for residents of the nearby hotel and apartment towers. As Nicolai Ouroussoff wrote in the *New York Times:*

> Such decisions could well determine whether Atlantic Yards will feel like a privileged enclave or belong to the community as a whole. One imagines what might have been possible if the city had the resources or the will to support such a vision. . . . For Brooklyn residents who oppose Atlantic Yards, the Gehry-Ratner partnership is a natural target. But much of their anger should focus on the city and federal governments, which are apparently delighted

to give developers responsibility for building and maintaining parks and pedestrian thoroughfares. That decision has changed the character of our cities as much as any single event in the past half century. Once commercial forces rule, such spaces are no longer really public."[84]

In an interview with Ouroussoff, Gehry stated that his prominence put him in an entirely different position with developers. They have to meet me as an equal," Gehry said. Nonetheless, when it came to the public green spaces, Piano and Gehry, both world-class architects, lost their battles with developers. On the other hand, there are good signs from other places. In Weil am Rhein, Germany, for example, the environmental research center and exhibition space, LFone Landesgartenschau, by Pritzker Prize-winning architect Zaha Hadid, is completely integrated with its surroundings. The circulation ramps dissolve imperceptibly into garden paths. The ground itself seems to lift up and expand into terraces. Hadid specifically aims for an architecture where all elements of a whole region—buildings, the natural world, and infrastructure—seamlessly connect in what she calls a whole "field."[85]

Even the average citizen recognizes that private ownership and public space are incompatible. When the city of Chicago closed Millennium Park for a private party recently, the general outrage was palpable. The natural world is an open and free world where we all feel equal. Experiencing this enhances the civility that nourishes a democracy.

Architecture is not only an aesthetic art or a utilitarian art at the service of builders. It is also a civic art. At this time in our history, architects and the landscape professionals on their design teams must reassert their role as protectors of the public realm. With the support of lawmakers and other officials they can do their job. Without it, city life will be impoverished.

This book describing developments in Chicago attempts to capture a propitious moment when these forces are, for the most part, well balanced. I also hope it engenders energy and optimism in the spirit of those who read it, and that it will be helpful to people responsible for the design of cities in years to come.

Although the ideal city will always be elusive—changing times will always give rise to new needs—aiming for a city where people have both nature and culture close at hand is a useful humanistic goal, worthy of the best efforts its citizens can muster. Shooting for that star brings us closer to it.

Selected Bibliography

Bach, Ira J., ed. *Chicago's Famous Buildings.* Third edition. Chicago: University of Chicago Press, 1980. For more recent buildings, see the fifth edition (2003) by Franz Schulze and Kevin Harrington.

Bachrach, Julia Sniderman. *City in a Garden: A Photographic History of Chicago's Parks.* Santa Fe, NM: Center for American Places, 2001.

———. "Ossian Cole Simonds: Conservation Ethic in the Prairie Style." In *Midwestern Landscape Architecture,* ed. William H. Tishler. Urbana: University of Illinois Press, 2000.

Bachrach, Julia Sniderman, and William R. Tippens. *A Breath of Fresh Air: Chicago's Neighborhood Parks of the Progressive Reform Era, 1900–1923.* Chicago: Chicago Public Library Special Collections Department, and the Chicago Park District, 1989.

Balmori, Diana, Diane Kostial McGuire, and Eleanor M. McPeck. *Beatrix Farrand's American Landscapes: Her Gardens and Campuses.* Millwood, NY: Sagapress, 1985.

Banham, Reyner. *Los Angeles: The Architecture of Four Ecologies.* New York: Harper & Row, 1971.

Bennett, Paul. "The Unmotor City." *Landscape Architecture Magazine,* March 1999

Birnbaum, Charles A., and Robin Karson, eds. *Pioneers of American Landscape Design.* New York: McGraw Hill, 2000.

Block, Jean F. *The Uses of Gothic: Planning and Building the Campus of the University of Chicago, 1892–1932.* Chicago: University of Chicago Library, 1983.

Bluestone, Daniel. *Constructing Chicago.* New Haven: Yale University Press, 1991.

Bruegmann, Robert. "The Art Institute Expands." *Museum Studies* 14, no. 1. Chicago: Art Institute of Chicago, 1988.

Burnham, Daniel H., and Edward H. Bennett. *The Plan of Chicago.* Chicago: Commercial Club, 1909.

Buisseret, David, ed. *Envisioning the City: Six Studies in Urban Cartography.* Chicago: University of Chicago Press, 1998.

Chappell, Sally A. Kitt. *Architecture and Planning of Graham, Anderson, Probst, and White: 1912–1936: Transforming Tradition.* Chicago: University of Chicago Press, 1992.

City of Chicago Department of Planning and Development. *Chicago River Corridor Development Plan.* 1999.

———. *Chicago River Corridor Design Guidelines and Standards.* 1999.

———. *Guide to the Chicago Landscape Ordinance. Regulations and guidelines relating to Title 10, Chapter 32 and Title 17, Chapter 194A of the Chicago Municipal Code.* 2000.

Clarke, Jane. "A Man for All Seasons." *Inland Architect,* July–August 1993.

Conzen, Michael P., ed. *The Making of the American Landscape.* New York: Routledge, 1990.

Corner, James, ed. *Recovering Landscape: Essays in Contemporary Landscape Architecture.* Princeton, NJ: Princeton Architectural Press, 1999.

Cranz, Galen. *The Politics of Park Design: A History of Urban Parks in*

America. Cambridge, MA: MIT Press, 1982.

Creese, Walter L. *The Crowning of the American Landscape: Eight Great Spaces and Their Buildings*. Princeton, NJ: Princeton University Press, 1985.

Cronon, William. *Nature's Metropolis: Chicago and the Great West*. New York: W. W. Norton, 1991.

Fabos, Julius Gy., Gordon T. Milde, and V. Michael Weinmayr. *Frederick Law Olmsted, Sr.: Founder of Landscape Architecture in America*. Amherst: University of Massachusetts Press, 1968.

Friends of the Chicago River, Northeastern Illinois Planning Commission, and City of Chicago Department of Planning and Development. *From Stockyards to Spawning Beds: A Handbook of Bank Restoration Designs for the Chicago River and other Urban Streams*. 1998.

Gerlach-Spriggs, Nancy, Richard Enoch Kaufman, and Sam Bass Warner Jr. *Restorative Gardens: The Healing Landscape*. New Haven: Yale University Press, 1998.

Grese, Robert E. *Jens Jensen: Maker of Natural Parks and Gardens*. Baltimore: Johns Hopkins University Press, 1992.

Harris, Dianne. *The Nature of Authority: Villa Culture, Landscape, and Representation in Eighteenth-Century Lombardy*. University Park: Pennsylvania State University Press, 2003.

Harris, Neil. "The Planning of the Plan." Pamphlet containing the text of Harris's speech to the Commercial Club of Chicago, November 27, 1979. Published by the club, in observance of the opening of the exhibition "The Plan of Chicago: 1909–1979," at the Art Institute of Chicago.

Hill, Libby. *The Chicago River: A Natural and Unnatural History*. Chicago: Lake Claremont Press, 2000.

Hiss, Tony. *The Experience of Place*. New York: Random House, 1991.

Holt, Glen E., and Dominic A. Pacyga. *Chicago: A Historical Guide to the Neighborhoods: The Loop and South Side*. Chicago: Chicago Historical Society, 1979.

Jacobs, Jane. *The Death and Life of Great American Cities*. New York: Random House, 1961.

Jellicoe, Geoffrey, and Susan Jellicoe. *The Landscape of Man: Shaping the Environment from Prehistory to the Present Day*. London: Thames and Hudson, 1975.

Johnson, Jory. With photographs by Felice Frankel. *Modern Landscape Architecture: Redefining the Garden*. New York: Abbeville Press, 1991.

Kostof, Spiro. *A History of Architecture: Settings and Rituals*. New York: Oxford University Press, 1985.

Lanctot, Barbara. *A Walk through Graceland Cemetery*. Chicago: Chicago Architecture Foundation, 1977.

Mayer, Harold M., and Richard C. Wade. *Chicago: Growth of a Metropolis*. Chicago: University of Chicago Press, 1969.

Meinig, D. W., ed. *The Interpretation of Ordinary Landscapes*. New York: Oxford University Press, 1979.

Mitchell, W. J. T., ed. *Landscape and Power*. Chicago: University of Chicago Press, 1994.

Newton, Norman T. *Design on the Land: The Development of Landscape Architecture*. Cambridge, MA: Harvard University Press, 1971.

Pacyga, Dominic A., and Ellen Skerrett. *Chicago: City of Neighborhoods*. Chicago: Loyola University Press, 1986.

Pridmore, Jay. *The University of Chicago: An Architectural Tour*. New York: Princeton Architectural Press, 2006.

Rainey, Reuben M. "William Le Baron Jenney and Chicago's West Parks." In *Midwestern Landscape Architecture*, ed. William H. Tischler. Urbana: University of Illinois Press, 2000.

Ranney, Victoria Post. *Olmsted in Chicago*. Chicago: Open Lands Project, 1972.

Rogers, Elizabeth Barlow. *Landscape Design: A Cultural and Architectural History*. New York: Harry N. Abrams, 2001.

Rotenberg, Robert, and Gary McDonogh, eds. *The Cultural Meaning of Urban Space*. Westport, CT: Bergin & Garvey: 1993.

Saunders, William S., ed. *Daniel Urban Kiley: The Early Gardens*. New York: Princeton Architectural Press, 1999.

Schaudt, Peter Lindsay. "Rehabilitation in Context: Alfred Caldwell's Planting Design for the Illinois Institute of Technology—Rediscovered and Interpreted." *Vineyard* 2, no. 1 (2000).

Schulze, Franz. *Illinois Institute of Technology: An Architectural Tour*. New York: Princeton Architectural Press, 2005.

Scully, Vincent. *Architecture: The Natural and the Manmade*. New York: St. Martin's Press, 1991.

Sinkevitch, Alice, ed. *AIA Guide to Chicago*. New York: Harcourt Brace, 1993.

Spirn, Anne Whiston. *The Granite Garden: Urban Nature and Human Design*. New York: Basic Books, 1984.

Stilgoe, John R. *Borderland: Origins of the American Suburb, 1820–1939*. New Haven: Yale University Press, 1988.

Tippens, William W. "Café Brauer." In *AIA Guide to Chicago*, ed. Alice Sinkevitch. New York: Harcourt Brace, 1993.

Tishler, William H. ed. *American Landscape Architecture: Designers and Places*. Washington, D.C.: Preservation Press, 1989.

Treib, Marc, ed. *Modern Landscape Architecture: A Critical Review*. Cambridge, MA: MIT Press, 1993.

Turner, Paul Venable. *Campus: An American Planning Tradition*. Cambridge, MA: MIT Press, 1984.

Vinci, John, and Stephen F. Christy, with Phillip Hamp. "Inventory and Evaluation of the Historic Parks in the City of Chicago." Unpublished manuscript. Available from the Chicago Park District archive.

Wille, Lois. *Forever Open, Clear, and Free: The Historic Struggle for Chicago's Lakefront*. First edition. Chicago: Henry Regnery, 1972.

———. *At Home in the Loop: How Clout and Community Built Chicago's Dearborn Park*. Carbondale: Southern Illinois University Press, 1997.

Illustration credits

Maps. Chicago CartoGraphics.

Figs. 1, 15, 36, 37, 42. Photos from Terry Evans, *Revealing Chicago: An Aerial Portrait* (New York: Harry N. Abrams, 2005).

Figs. 2, 16, 48, 51, 55; title page; pp. xxviii–xxix, 132–33. Photos from Robert Cameron, *Above Chicago* (San Francisco: Cameron, 1992).

Fig. 3. City of Chicago; Mark Farina, photographer.

Fig. 4. Douglass Hoerr Landscape Architecture, Inc.

Figs. 5, 6, 23. Karina Wang.

Fig. 7. William Kildow.

Figs. 8, 25; pp. 70–71. Jacobs/Ryan Associates.

Fig. 9. © 2004 Bruce Van Inwegen.

Figs. 10, 11. © The Art Institute of Chicago.

Figs. 12, 14, 20, 26, 33, 35, 46, 47, 56, 58, 65, 68, 76. Sally A. Kitt Chappell.

Figs. 13, 40, 41; pp. 18–19, 108–9. Chicago Park District; Brook Collins, photographer.

Fig. 17. Site Design Group, Ltd.

Figs. 18, 24. Les A. Boschke.

Figs. 19, 57. Steinkamp/Ballogg Photography.

Fig. 21. Chicago History Museum, negative ICHI-39145; Laszlo L. Kondor, photographer.

Fig. 22. © Hedrich-Blessing; Steve Hall, photographer.

Fig. 27. Diane Legge Kemp (DLK) Associates.

Fig. 28. Goettsch Partners.

Figs. 29, 62. Hedrich-Blessing.

Fig. 30; pp. 92–93. Gregory Murphey.

Fig. 31. © 2005 Chicago Tribune Company; Chuck Berman, photographer. All rights reserved.

Fig. 32. Chicago History Museum, negative HB-SN875-A; photo by Hedrich-Blessing.

Fig. 34. © The Museum of Modern Art. Licensed by SCALA/Art Resource, NY.

Figs. 38, 39, 44, 49, 60, 69, 71. Judith Bromley.

Fig. 43. University of Chicago Publications; Peter Kiar, photographer.

Figs. 45, 54, 66, 72, 73. Chicago Park District Special Collections.

Fig. 50. Conservation Design Forum.

Fig. 52. Wolff Landscape Architecture; William Kildow, photographer.

Fig. 53. Will Sumpter Associates; © 2006 Flip Chalfant, photographer.

Fig. 59; pp. 146–47. Lincoln Park Conservancy.

Fig. 61. Chicago History Museum, negative HB-00888-F2; photo by Hedrich-Blessing.

Figs. 74, 75. Chicago History Museum, negatives ICHI-29460, ICHI-04217.

Figs. 63, 64. Kimberly Pence.

Fig. 67; pp. 180–81. Michael LaCoste.

Fig. 70. © 2005 Robert Knapp.

Fig. 77. Marge Beaver, photographer.

Pp. 226–27. Chicago Botanic Garden; Bill Biderbost, photographer.

Notes

1. Nancy Stieber, "Learning from Interdisciplinarity," *Journal of the Society of Architectural Historians* 64, no. 4 (December 2005): 419–20.

2. Mario Carpo, "Architecture: Theory, Interdisciplinarity, and Methodological Eclecticism," *Journal of the Society of Architectural Historians* 64, no. 4 (December 2005): 425

3. Blair Kamin, "New Library Makes Success Look Simple," *Chicago Tribune*, April 2, 2006, sec. 7, 7.

4. Ibid., 6.

5. Martha Thorne, quoted in Robin Pogrebin, "Architect from Brazil Is Awarded the Pritzker," *New York Times*, April 10, 2006, B1.

6. Howard Reich, "How Millennium Park Created a Unique Nexus of Culture," *Chicago Tribune*, May 28, 2006, sec. 7, 1.

7. Hyde Park Historical Society and Community Task Force for Promontory Point, "Promontory Park in Burnham Park," July 13, 2003, 2, http://www.savethepoint.org.

8. Walter Hood, "Topologies/Typologies," lecture at the Graham Foundation for Advanced Studies in the Fine Arts, Chicago, March 1, 2006.

9. Sally Kitt Chappell, "Neighborhood Namesake: The Early History of Lincoln Park," *DePaul Magazine*, winter 1989, 11.

10. Jacqueline Burgess, Carolyn Harrison, and Melanie Limb, *People Parks and Urban Greens: A Study of Popular Meanings and Values for Open Spaces in the City* (London: Taylor & Francis Group, 1988), 460–62.

11. George Eliot, *The Mill on the Floss* (New York: A. L. Burt Company, n.d.), 41.

12. Interview, July 5, 2004. The woman asked not to be identified.

13. Neil Harris, "The Planning of the Plan," speech to the Commercial Club of Chicago, November 27, 1979. For how much of the plan was implemented, see Sally Chappell, "Chicago Issues: The Enduring Power of a Plan," in *The Plan of Chicago: 1909–1979*, ed. John Zukowsky, 6–15 (Chicago: Art Institute of Chicago, 1979).

14. Blair Kamin, "John Bryan: Millennium Park's Moneyman," *Chicago Tribune*, October 26, 2004, sec. 7, 3.

15. Ned Cramer, "Open Is Open," *Insights* (Chicago Architecture Foundation newsletter), spring 2006.

16. Trust for Public Land, http://www.tpl.org.

17. Keith Schneider, "To Revitalize a City, Try Spreading Some Mulch," *New York Times*, May 17, 2006, A6.

18. Streetscape project director Janet Attarian, telephone interview, 2004. See also http://cityofchicago.org., *City of Chicago Streetscape Guidelines*, 1–3.

19. Reich, "How Millennium Park Created a Unique Nexus," 1, 9.

20. Gary Washburn, "Cultural Center Rooftop Getting Garden of Its Own," *Chicago Tribune*, November 15, 2005, sect. 2, 1, 4.

21. "Chicago's Green Rooftops: A Guide to Rooftop Gardening," City of Chicago, Chicago Department of Environment, n.d.

22. Jane Clarke, interview, April 3, 2005.

23. Interview, July 30, 2004. The woman asked not to be identified.

24. John Handley, "Green Stretches Past Park: Park Adds Value to Surrounding Real Estate," *Chicago Tribune*, November 4, 2005, sec. 3, 1.

25. Constance Garrison, interview, July 2004.

26. Jane Clarke, "A Man for All Seasons," *Inland Architect*, July–August 1993, 64–68.

27. The title of Jane Clarke's previously cited article, "A Man for All Seasons," referred to landscape architect Dan Kiley.

28. Robert Bruegmann, "The Art Institute Expands: Challenges of Mid-Century," *Museum Studies* 14, no. 1 (1988): 74.

29. Paul Bennett, "The Unmotor City," *Landscape Architecture Magazine*, March 1999, 69–75, 100–102.

30. Sally A. Kitt Chappell, *Architecture and Planning of Graham, Anderson, Probst, and White, 1912–1936: Transforming Tradition* (Chicago: University of Chicago Press, 1992).

31. Lois Wille, *At Home in the Loop: How Clout and Community Built Chicago's Dearborn Park* (Carbondale: Southern Illinois University Press, 1997).

32. Daniel Weinbach, interview, January 20, 2006.

33. Libby Hill, *The Chicago River: A Natural and Unnatural History* (Chicago: Lake Claremont Press, 2000): 187–89.

34. Julia Sniderman Bachrach, *The City in a Garden: A Photographic History of Chicago's Parks.* (Santa Fe, NM: Center for American Places, 2001), 163.

35. Blair Kamin, "Wabash Plaza Could Be Start of Great Space," *Chicago Tribune*, November 6, 2005, sec. 7, 6.

36. Carol JH. Yetken, interview, May 20, 2005.

37. Ira J. Bach, *Chicago's Famous Buildings*, 3rd ed. (Chicago: University of Chicago Press, 1980): 182.

38. Peter Lindsay Schaudt, "Rehabilitation in Context: Alfred Caldwell's Planting Design for the Illinois Institute of Technology—Rediscovered and Interpreted," *Vineyard* 2, no. 1 (2000): 11–13.

39. Ibid.

40. Originally Jackson Park, the Midway Plaisance, and Washington Park were parts of Chicago's 1,055-acre South Park. The eastern section was renamed Jackson Park in 1880 in honor of Andrew Jackson, seventh president of the United States. Frederick Law Olmsted redesigned the grounds for the World's Columbian Exposition of 1893 and again after the fair, when his firm was officially Olmsted, Olmsted and Eliot. After 1900 the Olmsted Brothers also consulted on the landfill near Sixty-third Street.

41. Neil Harris, "University of Chicago Campus," in *AIA Guide to Chicago*, ed. Alice Sinkevitch (New York: Harcourt Brace, 1993).

42. Jean F. Block, *The Uses of Gothic: Planning and Building the Campus of the University of Chicago, 1892–1932* (Chicago: University of Chicago Library, 1983), appendix, 195. Elsewhere Block identifies the various architects of the quadrangles: Henry Ives Cobb, Shepley, Rutan & Coolidge, Dwight H. Perkins, Charles Z. Klauder, and Coolidge & Hodgdon. Landscape architects listed include O. C. Simonds, John C. Olmsted, and Beatrix Farrand.

43. Olmsted Brothers, "Report to the Trustees," March 20, 1902, 33. Quoted in Block, *Uses of Gothic*, 195.

44. Diana Balmori, Diane Kostial McGuire, and Eleanor M. McPeck, *Beatrix Farrand's American Landscapes: Her Gardens & Campuses* (Millwood, NY: Sagapress, 1985), 130.

45. Ibid., 131.

46. Bachrach, *City in a Garden* 137.

47. Interview, Kevin M. Fitzgerald, golf professional, Harborside International, November 4, 2005; press releases written by John Gavin, August 2, 1995, November 14, 1995, and April 18, 1999.

48. Dominic A. Pacyga and Ellen Skerrett, *Chicago: City of Neighborhoods* (Chicago: Loyola University Press, 1986), 432.

49. Bachrach, *City in a Garden,* 69.

50. Barbara Lanctot, *A Walk through Graceland Cemetery* (Chicago: Chicago Architecture Foundation, 1977), 2. See also Julia Sniderman Bachrach, "Ossian Cole Simonds: Conservation Ethic in the Prairie Style," in *Midwestern Landscape Architecture,* ed. William H. Tishler (Urbana: University of Illinois Press, 2000).

51. Ken Fidel, interview, 1990.

52. "Montrose Beach Designated High-Quality Natural Area," *Friends of the Parks Advocate* fall 2005, 8.

53. National Geographic Guide to Bird Watching Sites: Eastern United States, Web site.

54. Lois Wille, *Forever Open, Clear, and Free: The Historic Struggle for Chicago's Lakefront,* 1st ed. (Chicago: Henry Regnery, 1972).

55. William W. Tippens, "Café Brauer," in Sinkevitch, *AIA Guide to Chicago.*

56. Deborah Vaughan, interview, February 8, 2006; Thomas Beebe, interview, March 29, 2006.

57. Donors and the list of people who worked to obtain gifts include Tim Samuelson, Walter Creese, Nell McClure, Elaine Harrington, Don Hackl, Richard Pepper, John Zukowsky, Pauline Saliga, and Willard Boyd.

58. Daniel Bluestone, *Constructing Chicago* (New Haven: Yale University Press, 1991), 216n 80 (citing an article in the *Chicago Tribune,* July 6, 1873).

59. Ibid., 57.

60. Quoted in "The Public Parks of Chicago, Their Origin, Former Control and Present Government," *Chicago City Manual, 1914* (Chicago: City of Chicago, 1914), 7. I owe this reference to Julia Sniderman Bachrach.

61. Bluestone, *Constructing Chicago,* 54.

62. Daniel H. Burnham and Edward H. Bennett, *Plan of Chicago,* ed. Charles Moore (Chicago: Da Capo, 1970), plate 103.

63. Pacyga and Skerrett, *Chicago.*

64. Reuben M. Rainey, "William Le Baron Jenney and Chicago's West Parks," in *Midwestern Landscape Architecture,* ed. William H. Tischler, (Urbana: University of Illinois Press, 2000), 65. Rainey's principal sources are the first, second, and third annual reports of the West Chicago Park Commission.

65. Ibid., 67.

66. John Vinci and Stephen F. Christy, with Phillip Hamp, *Inventory and Evaluation of the Historic Parks in the City of Chicago.* No page numbers are in this unpublished manuscript, which lists the parks in alphabetical order.

67. A Viennese example would be a design by Franz Lebisch (1908) appearing in Robert Rotenberg, *Landscape and Power in Vienna* (Baltimore: Johns Hopkins University Press, 1995), 160. Still extant are the Wienportal in the Stadtpark and the Kaiserin Elizabeth Memorial in the Volksgarten. See also Robert E. Grese, *Jens Jensen: Maker of Natural Parks and Gardens,* (Baltimore: Johns Hopkins University Press, 1992), 80.

68. Quoted in Grese, *Jens Jensen,* 80.

69. Burgess, Harrison, and Limb, *People Parks and Urban Greens,* 472.

70. Included in the exhibition were projects at the Chicago Public Library at 3030 West Fullerton Avenue; North Lawndale; Cook County Jail Garden, Twenty-sixth Street and California Avenue (not accessible to visitors without prior arrangement); Garfield Park Conservatory Demonstration Garden; El Coqui, Crystal Street and Rockwell Avenue; El Jardin de las Mariposas, Eighteenth and Carpenter Streets, in the Pilsen neighborhood; Elliott Donnelley Youth Center, Thirty-ninth Street and Michigan

Avenue; Faraday Elementary School, Monroe Street and Kedzie Avenue; Howard Area Community Garden, Juneway Terrace and Hermitage Avenue; Slumbusters Garden, Twenty-first Street and Trumbull Avenue; CHA Stateway Gardens, at Thirty-sixth and State Streets; Turn a Lot Around Gardens (four gardens), Forty-eighth Forty-ninth Streets on Wabash Avenue, and Forty-third Street and Martin Luther King Jr. Drive; Grand Boulevard; and Hay Community Academy, Laramie Avenue and Augusta Boulevard.

71. Bachrach, *City in a Garden,* 77.

72. Quoted in Vinci, Christy, and Hamp, *Historic Parks,* Washington Park conclusion.

73. http://www.uchicago.edu/docs/mp-site/plaisanceplan; accessed September 14, 2004.

74. Sarah Whiting, "Bas-Relief Urbanism: Chicago's Figured Field," in *Mies in America,* ed. Phyllis Lambert (New York: Henry N. Abrams, 2001), 642–91.

75. Nicholas Adams, unpublished manuscript on Skidmore, Owings & Merrill. Robert Bruegmann kindly alerted me to this work.

76. Katherine DePriest, archivist for Skimore, Owings & Merrill, found the information on the landscape architect for this project.

77. Walter Netsch, interview, January 18, 2006.

78. Andrea Faber Taylor, Frances E. Kuo, and William C. Sullivan, "Views of Nature and Self-Discipline: Evidence from Inner City Children, *Journal of Environmental Psychology* 22 (2002): 49–63; Kuo, "Coping with Poverty: Impacts of Environment on Attention in the Inner City," *Environment and Behavior,* January 2002, 5–34; Kuo and Sullivan, "Aggression and Violence in the Inner City: Effects of Environment on Mental Fatigue," *Environment and Behavior,* July 2001, 543; Kuo and Sullivan, "Environment and Crime in the Inner City: Does Vegetation Reduce Crime?" *Environment and Behavior* 33, no. 3 (May 2001): 343–67; Kuo, Sullivan, Rebekah Leving Coley, and Lisette Brunson, "Fertile Ground for Community: Inner-City Neighborhood Common Spaces," *American Journal of Community Psychology* 26, no. 6 (1998): 823; Rebekah Levine Coley, Kuo, and Sullivan, "Where Does Community Grow? The Social Context Created by Nature in Urban Public Housing," *Environment and Behavior* 29, no. 4 (July 1997): 468–94. Another useful reference is Lee Rainwater, *Behind Ghetto Walls: Black Families in a Ghetto Slum* (Chicago: Aldine, 1970).

79. Interview, August 27, 2005. The woman asked not to be indentified.

80. Sheila Brady and Lisa E. Delplace, "Homage to the Prairie," *Landscape Architecture Magazine,* September 2003, 20–26.

81. The trees are accolade elms, a disease-resistant type that the Chicago Botanic Garden acquired years ago and nurtured until they reached their majestic size today.

82. *Chicago Tonight,* WTTW television, February 13, 2006.

83. *New Designs for Public Spaces: Millennium Park and Beyond,* exhibition at the Chicago Architecture Foundation, winter 2005–2006.

84. Nicholai Ouroussoff, "Skyline for Sale," *New York Times,* June 4, 2006, sec. 2, 37.

85. Monica Ramirez-Montagut, *Zaha Hadid: Thirty Years in Architecture* (guide accompanying the exhibition *Zaha Hadid,* June 3–October 25, 2006, at the Solomon R. Guggenheim Museum, New York), 5–7.

Index

NOTE: Bracketed numbers in **bold** indicate entry numbers. Numbers in *italics* indicate maps.

Mokena Community
Public Library District